OVER THE RAINBOW:
HOW GOD'S RAINBOW PROMISE IS BEING
FULFILLED IN RURAL NICARAGUA

THE RAINBOW NETWORK STORY

OVER THE RAINBOW:

How God's Rainbow Promise is Being Fulfilled in Rural Nicaragua

By
Linda Leicht

Photography by
Steve Sonheim

Discussion Questions by
Rev. William Moore

Quiet Waters Publications

Bolivar, Missouri
2017

Quiet Waters Publications
P.O. Box 34, Bolivar, MO 65613-0034 USA
www.quietwaterspub.com

Photography: Steve Sonheim
Cover Design: Sam Trobisch

ISBN 978-1-931475-66-2
Library of Congress
Control Number: 2017927967

Acknowledgements

Writing this book has been a life-changing experience. I had often written about Rainbow Network and the amazing work they do in Nicaragua when I was a journalist. I even visited Nicaragua to write about it in 2004.

So, when Keith Jaspers asked me to prayerfully consider writing a book for the organization, I was definitely intrigued. But work and family and all the vagaries of life seemed to get in the way until 2015, when I had retired from journalism and was working for a local food bank. That was when Keith called again.

God's timing is always impeccable. I was not feeling fulfilled in my new job, and my nonagenarian mother had moved in with me. I needed to spend more time at home, and I needed to do something that had meaning for me.

Rainbow Network provided that. I hope that this book is as meaningful to the organization, its supporters, and all those people who might stumble across it and maybe be moved to become supporters.

Keith isn't the only one I need to thank. Megan Munzlinger, Rainbow's Development Director and Number One Cheerleader, helped me to get to know the people I would meet in Nicaragua, was often my traveling companion and translator and even took me zip lining for the first time in my 67 years. Megan has such a deep love for Nicaragua and Rainbow Network. Her devotion to that cause and to God's call are inspiring to all who meet her.

Photographer and Rainbow supporter Steve Sonheim was not only a pleasure to meet and work with; he is also an extraordinary talent. His photos make the stories in this book come alive. And his open and genuine embrace of all things Nicaragua has been a challenge to me to be more willing to step outside of my own comfort zone and experience God's miraculous creation wherever I am.

Dr. Bill Moore provided the thoughtful and thought provoking discussion questions at the end of the chapters in each of the four ministry areas. His deep faith and love for this ministry are evident in this project and all his amazing support.

Our translators Mayra Samteliz, Jairo Cortez and Eliud Rivera were not only my ears and voice in Nicaragua, they were a true part of the community. I saw Eliud reach down to help a child as if he were his own. Jairo became a friend to me and to all the volunteers, medical staff and church visitors in ways that made us all feel welcome and at home. I especially want to thank him for giving me a copy of the book "Blood of Brothers," which gave me such insight into the soul of his country. Mayra showed me what is possible in Nicaragua when families have the resources and support to raise healthy, educated children who will someday lead this wonderful country.

I spoke with so many people who touched me with their stories, but a few will remain in my heart forever. Sarah Janellis is a teenager who embraces life with a hold so tight she squeezes everything she can get out of it. Sarah's story is in the health section, but her story is not over. She will do and be something amazing in the years to come.

Alba de los Angeles Calero is one of my heroes. Her determination and sweet spirit have brought education to so many children in her little community. I will never forget the day we stepped into that tiny, dark school room where her students greeted us with a song. Now, she teaches in a brand new building with light pouring in just like the Rainbow light she brings them with their lessons each day.

Angela Centeno is the true spirit of leadership and love. Despite the terrible loss of her daughter, Margine, she leads the people of her community and always keeps her head up high. She cares so much about her neighbors, and they love her in return. She is an amazing example for younger women – everywhere.

Manuel Alegria taught me that laughter and joy are the most important part of success. He is a born businessman and leader, but this tiny man in a bright green pickup truck understands the business of a smile, too. He took us on an arduous climb on a hot day just to see his bean field, then entertained us along the way back with a little jig as we sat in the shade to catch our breath. Thank you, Manuel, and your wonderful family for your hospitality and humor.

I loved meeting many others on my journeys to Nicaragua with Rainbow Network, but I cannot mention them all here. I want each person who shared their story with me, who helped me get around, who gave me food and drinks and love – from the wait staff at the hotels to the children who laughed at my sorry attempts to speak Spanish – to know that they have all touched and changed my life.

Most of all, I want to thank God for putting me in this story and for sending me to rural Nicaragua to find the face of Jesus in so many people. I thank God for all my blessings, but I also thank God for showing me that blessings don't always come with a price tag. Like Manuel's jig, some of the best blessings are freely given.

Linda Leicht
Springfield, MO

Linda Leicht is an award-winning newspaper and magazine journalist. Before retiring in 2014, she worked for 36 years in Arkansas and Missouri, covering a wide range of topics, including religion and nonprofits. She now works part-time as a freelance writer.

Table of Contents

Acknowledgements i

God Sent A Rainbow

Chapter One:

Living the Rainbow 9
Answer to Prayers 10
Finding Nicaragua 10

Housing

Chapter Two:

La Corona Views 15
Something to Think About 19

Chapter Three:

The Difference a House Makes 21
An Answer to Prayer 22
Determination and Faith 24
From Homeless to Homeowner 25
Sent by God 26
Given a Chance 26
Something to Think About 28

Chapter Four:

Learning to Serve 31
Something to Think About 33

Chapter Five:

How It Works 35
Success in Los Pinos 37
Something to Think About 39

Chapter Six

How You Can Help 41
Something to Think About 45

Healthcare

Chapter Seven

The Lame Shall Walk 47

Inspiration in a First Step 49

As Long as the Lord Provides 51

Something to Think About 53

Chapter Eight:

The Blind Shall See 55

Seeing the Future...57

Something to Think About 59

Chapter Nine:

A Good Doctor 61

Something to Think About 63

Chapter Ten:

How It Works..65

Responding to Starvation 67

Miracles Found in Tragedy 68

Something to Think About 70

Chapter Eleven:

How You Can Help 71

Something to Think About 74

Education

Chapter Twelve:

Changing Lives and Communities 77

Fulfilling Your Destiny...79

Giving Back to Your Community 80

Never Giving Up...82

Something to Think About 83

Chapter Thirteen

Caring for Orphans..85

Sharing Your Story...86

Returning the Favor 87

A Happy Heart 88
A Heart to Help 88
Something to Think About 89

Chapter Fourteen

A Word of Hope 91
Something to Think About 93

Chapter Fifteen:

How It Works 95
Something to Think About 99

Chapter Sixteen:

How You Can Help 101
Something to Think About 103

Economic Development

Chapter Seventeen:

Learning to Succeed 105
Dinner at Hairy's 107
Rancher, Businessman, Father, Leader 109
Something to Think About 111

Chapter Eighteen:

Changing Lives 113
Looking at the Future 114
Spiritual Revival 115
Something to Think About 118

Chapter Nineteen:

A Perfect Match...121
Something to Think About 123

Chapter Twenty:

How It Works 125
Something to Think About 128

Chapter Twenty-One:

How You Can Help 129
Something to Think About...131

The Future of Rainbow

Chapter Twenty-Two:

Doubling God's Blessings..133

Chapter Twenty-Three:

How It Works..135

Chapter Twenty-Four:

On Board with Rainbow 139

Chapter Twenty-Five:

Learning to be a Leader...143

Chapter Twenty-Six:

Rainbow Network's History 147
Sharing Success...149
Feeding the Hungry 152

Chapter Twenty-Seven:

How You Can Help 157

God Sent a Rainbow

I have set my rainbow in the clouds, and it will be the sign
of the covenant between me and the earth.

Genesis 9:13

Rainbow Network's Nicaragua Director Nelson Palacios welcomes
some mothers and children to the medical clinic at El Carmen.

CHAPTER ONE

LIVING THE RAINBOW

The lanes that crisscross the community of El Carmen are lined with tall greenery and bright orange flowers between the road and solid concrete block houses with sturdy metal roofs.

The children who run up and down the lanes to school and play have bright brown eyes and shiny black hair. The mothers cook in airy kitchens that allow the smoke from their cook stoves to vent outside instead of settling in the family's lungs. Colorful gardens fill backyards and grow along pathways.

Small home-based stores – *pulperias* – dot the community. Bakeries, eateries, small manufacturing, taxis, sewing cooperatives and other businesses make El Carmen a vibrant, successful community. Income from those ventures pay for food, education, medical care, clothing, basic necessities and even fun entertainment.

This is a Rainbow Network community. Little more than a decade ago, before Rainbow Network arrived, the residents of this hillside high in the mountains of rural Nicaragua lived in shacks, made from scrap wood, metal, paper and plastic. Children's eyes were sad and frightened, their hair dull, and their skin often broken out in rashes and sores. Mothers stood over pots of boiling plantains, the only dinner available. Despondent and hopeless fathers were often absent, having left their families in search of work after depressed coffee prices closed large corporate coffee plantations that once offered wages, scant as they were, for their back-breaking labor.

Ask the people of El Carmen about that change and they are quick to call it an answer to their prayers. These deeply faithful people had been praying to God for a way to help their children escape the poverty, disease and despair that entrapped this beautiful place in the mountains of the Matagalpa region.

"God sent Rainbow Network," they will tell you.

* * *

Answer to Prayers

When Keith and Karen Jaspers started Rainbow Network in 1995, they had also been praying for an answer. They prayed for a way that they could change lives in a place where no one else was stepping up to help. They wanted to invest their own money in God's work, so they prayed for direction. God sent them to Nicaragua.

Nicaragua is a beautiful tropical country in Central America, nestled between Honduras and Costa Rica, with long coastlines on both the Pacific Ocean and the Caribbean Sea. Settled by the Spanish on the West Coast and the British on the East Coast, Nicaragua became an independent country in 1821.

Despite being rich in such metals as gold, silver, tungsten, zinc, copper and lead, the country has natural environmental challenges, including mudslides, hurricanes and earthquakes.

By the 1970s, the country was governed by a cruel and corrupt government, which ultimately led to a revolution that ushered in a Marxist government, the Sandinistas, in 1979. This conflict brought on a U.S.-backed opposition – the Contras – that kept the country in devastating civil war and a state of unrest for the next decade. The war and unrest took a terrible toll on the country's economy, especially on its poor. Then, in 1998, Hurricane Mitch struck.

* * *

Finding Nicaragua

God needed a servant to step in and help His children in this beautiful but broken place. Keith and Karen Jaspers answered that call.

The Jaspers grew up in rural Iowa, children of simple farmers. They used the lessons of industry and determination they learned in their youth to start businesses that eventually brought their family wealth. But before they earned that success, they had agreed that if they succeeded financially they would use their wealth to help others.

After reading the book "Love In The Mortar Joints" by Habitat for Humanity founder Millard Fuller, Keith and Karen drove all the way to Americus, Ga., to meet this man and learn more about the organization. Eventually, Keith served on the board of directors of Habitat for Humanity International alongside former President Jimmy Carter.

It was their work with Habitat for Humanity that taught them the lessons necessary to envision Rainbow Network, an organization that offers a holistic approach to helping families raise themselves out of poverty. When they saw the need in Nicaragua, they knew that God had led them where they were to do the work.

It started small, in only a few communities near the capital city of Managua, focusing on providing housing, using the Habitat for Humanity model of sweat equity and non-interest loans. God opened more doors, introducing more communities and demonstrating more ways to touch and change lives. Soon Rainbow Network added medical care, educational opportunities and economic development to ensure that each community had the needed resources to find its own way out of poverty.

After 20 years, Rainbow Network is active in more than 140 communities. With a Nicaraguan staff of about 40, Rainbow Network has built more than 1,000 homes, educated more than 50,000 children and adults, made it possible for people to start and grow businesses through more than 94,000 micro-loans, served more than 50 million meals to children, pregnant and nursing mothers and the elderly, and saved countless lives through medical care to more than 705,000 patients.

The principles of Rainbow Network are simple. People must be responsible for their own lives, so Rainbow Network makes it possible for the people in their "networks" to succeed. This book will tell the stories of many of those people: children who were dying of malnutrition who ultimately became college graduates, simple field workers who became successful entrepreneurs, mothers who became community leaders, and illiterate children who became teachers.

These are the stories of God's children and the miracles he brought to Nicaragua. These are stories that will encourage and enlighten. They will show you how God uses Rainbow Network and how you can be a part of this incredible work.

Housing

My people will abide in a peaceful habitation,
in secure dwellings and in quiet resting.

Isaiah 32:18

Keith Jaspers (right) talks with Millard Fuller, founder of Habitat for Humanity, during a visit in 2004. Keith's work with Habitat helped him develop Rainbow Network's housing program.

High in the mountains of Matagalpa, the La Corona housing project – seen here in the middle of construction – offers spectacular views, but for the new residents, it is the security of a home with a floor and roof that matters most.

CHAPTER TWO

LA CORONA VIEWS

The hillside at La Corona is filled with colorful balloons and palms in front of 25 simple concrete block homes that will soon be filled with excited families. Those families, as well as people from the village, the surrounding villages and cities, even from the United States, mill around where the plastic chairs are neatly arranged under blue and yellow frame tents.

This is a very special event in the life of the residents of La Corona in the municipality of San Ramon. Families who have been living with relatives or living in houses made of sticks and mud, black plastic sheeting and salvaged tin roofs that leak and turn the dirt floors into mud, will soon receive the keys to their new homes – homes that are safe and dry and their own.

These homes are a miracle for their new owners, and they are a miracle for Rainbow Network. They represent 1,000 homes that have been built thanks to the efforts of supporters from around the United States and the hard work of the people of rural Nicaragua.

The new houses were built over the course of six months by the future homeowners and their families. The funding for the homes was provided by the people of Woods Chapel United Methodist Church in Lees Summit, Missouri. Some of those church members are here for the big celebration, given places of honor under the speakers' tent.

The new housing project is located next to a previous project. Each new home is simple, concrete block, with a metal roof and covered front porch. There are secure, locked doors in the front and back, and windows to allow a breeze. A single large room inside, with a cement floor, the home will soon be filled with a family's belongings. Walls will go up to separate the rooms. A kitchen will be built out back to keep the smoke from entering the house and the family's lungs. A latrine at the back of each home's property is just waiting for the family to erect the metal walls for privacy.

The new houses look stark on this cleared hillside, but the pink, red, green, orange, and blue balloons as well as the stalks of palms tied to the porch poles predict what is to come. A glance over to the earlier project, just a year old, reveals lush greenery and colorful flowers growing around each house. Added rooms, gardens, personal touches and decorations make each house a home for the families inside.

The views from the hillside are stunning. The mountains roll with varying shades of green caused by trees, bushes, grass and moss. The houses at the top of the hillside have the best views, which would cost many thousands of dollars in the United States, but these simple homes come with it at no extra fee!

Clouds caress the mountain tops to keep the sun from the heads of the milling crowd as they wait for the program to begin with a welcome speech from one of the community leaders. He reads from Psalm 127, "Unless the Lord builds the house, the builders labor in vain." A local pastor blesses the houses and prays for blessings for the Rainbow Network supporters who came from so far away.

"These are dreams come true," says Eddy Sandino, Rainbow Network's San Ramon director. "You are the reason," he tells the supporters. This is the most recent of eight such housing projects in the San Ramon Network, and all of these houses are changing the lives of poor, rural Nicaraguan families – an answer to their prayers.

"By wisdom a house is built, and through understanding, it is established," a community leader reads from Proverbs.

The ceremony continues with traditional folk dances in costumes. The young, raven-haired women wear long, full white satin skirts and peasant blouses with gold sashes. Their fingers loop through the skirts to sweep them up and around as they dance. They have braided flowers in their hair with colorful ribbons. The young men are proud in their white and green suits and straw hats. The music is lively and the dances are rich in history, drawing the audience into their rhythms.

Sandra Picado Rodriguez is dressed in a beautiful black lace blouse as she steps up to the microphone. She and her family will receive the keys to their new home in just a few minutes, but she wants to say a few words first. She thanks God, "our fountain of life," then she thanks Rainbow Network. "You have made this wonderful housing project possible so we can have a home," she says in a clear, confident voice. "This is so important to us. ... Thank you for the love. ... The Bible says you cannot do works without faith. You are doing both."

Then she turns to the visitors from Missouri behind her. Looking into their eyes, she says that she hopes they can continue to help other communities as they have helped hers.

There are more prayers and Bible verses. Two little boys, who will also be moving into their new homes today, sing in English, "I'm waiting on You, Lord." One sings so loud it hurts your ears, but the boy is truly "bold and confident," as the song says, and the audience gives them a big round of applause.

Rainbow's Nicaragua director, Nelson Palacios, steps up indicating that the ceremony is nearly over and the families will soon get their keys. First, he asks God to bless the families. "Today you are going to start a new life in this community when you get a key and a Bible to guide your steps," he says. He thanks all the supporters who are there – a medical team led by Dr. Will Moore, a board member who has volunteered there for 15 years, board member Johnny Moneymaker, who helped to purchase the land for the project, and the members of Woods Chapel. "You are making many miracles here," he tells them.

He tells the community that Rainbow Network has been working together with them for 20 years "to get rid of poverty." He promises, "We will continue going forward. We will always be with you."

Megan Munzlinger, Rainbow Network's U.S. director, thanks the community for their welcome and their participation. "You put in hard work," she says. "We cannot wait to come back and see you prosper."

Pastor Mike Scott of Woods Chapel greets the crowd. "Today you have shown us God's love," he says. "Thank you, and God bless."

Then the mayor of San Ramon speaks, promising to bring electricity to the new housing project. "This is only possible with the love for God and others," he says.

Finally, it is time to hand out the keys, just as the clouds lift off the mountain tops to reveal a stunningly blue sky – a prophetic sign.

Each family steps up and selects one of the colorful collages hanging from strings around the speakers' tent. In it, is the number of their new home. Sandra Picado Rodriguez gets Number 21, about halfway down the hillside. She and her husband and four children will soon sleep in their own home. They take their key and Bible and head down to check out their house, accepting congratulations from their neighbors as they make their way down the hill. They are all smiles.

Son Jason Kennedy, 9, carries his New Testament as they step up onto the front porch. He smiles shyly but says he is very happy about his new home. The first thing he plans to do is plant a garden.

After an official ribbon-cutting at the top of the hill, everyone gets to unlock their doors and go into their own homes. Then they all eat, like a celebration in the United States – except that this meal is a simple bowl of rice and a piece of bread.

La Corona is much like the 34 other housing projects Rainbow Network has helped make a reality in the past 20 years – as will be the five more that were completed in 2016. There, people form community and work together to improve both their lives and their country. Because of supporters of Rainbow Network and all the people who believe in this work, all 1,000 houses built represent families who now have access to healthcare, nutrition, education and economic opportunity.

That is what it means to share the love of Jesus Christ in rural Nicaragua.

Something to Think About

(The following discussion questions would be appropriate for youth or adult groups.)

Read: James 2:14-26

1. Can you think of a frightening time when you had to act in faith? Explain.
2. Are you a "doer" or a "thinker"?
3. Does faith itself ever lead to saving results? Explain.
4. Do you think that faith leads to works of service? Explain.
5. Do you agree with James in verse 26 that faith without works is dead?
6. If you were arrested for being a Christian, what evidence would there be to convict you?
7. Is faith broken that does not result in works? Explain.
8. How can the Rainbow Network be an outlet for faithful action? Give specifics.

This "house" in La Grecia is the type of shelter many families in rural Nicaragua call home. Using the Habitat for Humanity model, Rainbow Network participants build and pay for safe, secure homes in their community.

The Rainbow Facts
Based on an average of eight people living in each house, more than 8,000 people in rural Nicaragua now have safe, secure housing, thanks to Rainbow Network.

CHAPTER THREE

THE DIFFERENCE A HOUSE MAKES

The housing program is a key element of the Rainbow Network philosophy and program. It was Keith Jaspers' involvement in Habitat for Humanity International that taught him how important it is for someone to have safe, secure housing as they find their way out of poverty. The privilege of owning a home is the first step in a life of dignity.

The homes in rural Nicaragua are typically small, often with a dirt floor and a simple tin roof. But many of the people Rainbow Network reaches would consider such a home to be a mansion. Building materials used in these isolated communities are not the bricks and lumber people in the United States would assume. They are sticks gathered in the woods, woven together to support a mud wall or to hold black plastic sheeting. Any piece of salvaged wood, plastic, metal or even newspaper can be utilized to secure a wall or roof.

Keith tells the story of asking a woman in Cuajachillo what she likes most about her new Rainbow house. She answered, "Two things. First, we used to get wet from two directions when it rained, and now we stay dry. Second, we have a solid door we can close and even lock." He didn't understand what she meant by getting wet from two directions until she explained that during the rainy season, when it is the norm to have hard rains nearly every day, water would run into the house on the dirt – now mud – floor from the sides because there was no foundation in their dirt floor hut. Moreover, water would pour in from several very bad leaks on the roof!

The powerful storms that come most afternoons during the rainy season can wash a mud hut away and powerful winds can send the scraps of materials used to secure a home flying like the Big Bad Wolf did with the Three Little Pigs' house of straw. The earthquakes common to this region often cause these stick houses to tumble to the ground.

But a Rainbow house is dry and safe during those storms. The metal roof is secured tightly to keep both the rain and the wind at bay, and the floors, built on a solid foundation, stay dry when the doors and windows are closed. The concrete block walls are strengthened with rebar to withstand the rumbling earthquakes.

It is important to remember, however, that Rainbow homes are not just built to withstand the verities of nature. They are intended to build up people and communities. They lift up the dignity of the families who live in them, the entire community and even the areas around the community.

When the houses that make up El Carmen, at the top of a mountain in Matagalpa, were first built more than a decade ago, they stood out like an oasis in a barren desert. The only homes nearby were dark, dank shanties where desperate mothers boiled unripe plantains on wood-burning stoves that filled the small rooms with toxic smoke so children's stomachs could be filled with a broth that barely kept them alive.

Today, the bustling community of El Carmen is filled with colorful houses surrounded by lush gardens. The roads are arteries for bicycles that carry busy adults and healthy children to work and school. There are stores where neighbors can buy food and household items businesses that provide employment and services. Nearby, more communities have sprung up and more businesses are flourishing.

This is an example of success breeding success, something Rainbow Network sees everyday.

That is what happened for Rufina Leonor Torres.

* * *

An Answer to Prayer

Rufina was only 6 years old when she was forced to go out on the street and sell bread and candy to be able to feed herself. Her mother died when she was only a baby, and her father remarried a woman with five children of her own and had four more with him. She did not want to raise the little girl, so Rufina lived with relatives who exploited her. They forced her to work hard and stop going to school after the fourth grade.

Still a child herself, when her father's marriage ended, Rufina agreed to raise her younger half-siblings. She took a job cleaning houses in the morning and made tortillas in the afternoon. With the money she earned and the little her father could contribute, she was able to buy food and second-hand clothing for her three brothers and one sister. When she was just 16, her father died, leaving her in charge of the little family. "I felt that the world was against me," Rufina recalled. "So I took that responsibility on me."

By 2005, at the age of 23, Rufina was desperate. She worried about her siblings, who had then moved back with their mother but were being abused. While visiting them in the little community of Ilego near Nagarote, her 13-year-old brother begged to return to live with her, but she was working all day in Managua and renting a room there. "If we could only have a house, even a plastic house, my life would be different," she thought.

It was Dec. 31 when she went to a church for a midnight service. The pastor gave her a blank sheet of paper and told her to write down what she would request of the Lord. She wrote, "a house."

In February, she learned about Rainbow Network as she desperately searched for a way to get a house. Rainbow was already building the Colonia Silvio Mayorga housing project in the Nagarote Network. She filled out an application, but the housing committee turned her down because she was young and single and had a future ahead of her. But with a little support from a cousin and a mason who was working on the housing project, she was encouraged to write her story and turn it in to the Network office. "Then I prayed, and I looked for the office," she recalled. "Nobody was there, just a doctor. I left the letter with the doctor and left to go to work."

A few weeks later, she learned the good news. She was accepted. "It was a very huge happiness." She quit her job and moved to Nagarote where she started selling fruit and vegetables, just about anything to earn a meager living. She worked on the housing project, and eventually she and her siblings were able to move into their new home.

"Rainbow Network has been a great support," she says, adding that her family has also been the recipient of scholarships and micro loans. "To them, I have been special."

With four mouths to feed, a house loan and utilities to pay, she ran a small store out of her house and also had a job. The Rainbow staff gave her a sewing machine, and she began making clothing and tablecloths to sell. "Then, Mr. Keith told them, 'You should pay for a sewing course.' I was able to learn more skills. Now I am a dressmaker for the housing project. I make uniforms for school."

She was then able to take a cake-making course, and now makes cakes, bread, doughnuts and other treats to sell in the community. And she even graduated from high school!

"I always inspire other people to do what I'm doing," she says with pride. "I always create competition. That's how you learn. So I said to myself, God is using me as an inspiration to others." Sometimes she is even able to hire some of her neighbors!

Her brothers and sister are all grown up now, married and have babies of their own. "They are always grateful for what I did for them," she says. "Whenever we see each other, we are so happy."

Rufina also has her own family now. She is married and has a 3-year-old daughter, Junaeisy Rostran. Her husband sometimes gets work in Managua, but when he is not employed, he works with her at home.

"I live a blessed life," Rufina says with confidence. "My life totally changed. It turned around completely."

When her father died, she was devastated, but she held Psalm 27:10 in her heart. "Though my father and mother forsake me, the Lord will receive me."

"I have always struggled," she acknowledged. "But I have always put my faith in God."

* * *

Determination and Faith

There are many more stories of lives changed thanks to a Rainbow home.

Jania Marlene Zeledon lives with her husband, Sergio Rocha, and their children in a home in the El Paraiso community. But when Rainbow Network arrived a dozen years ago, a group of about 25 families organized to ask for a much needed housing project. They were able to get land donated, and Jania became a leader in the community.

"It was such hard work," she says. "It was very tough to organize, but at the end of the day, we were able to reach our objectives. We are so happy because we have a roof to live under."

Thanks to Rainbow Network microloans, Jania and her family have been able to achieve much more than that, too. They have a small store in their home and are able to sell produce from their garden. With the profits, they were able to buy a truck, which her husband uses to drive to work at the coffee plantation and to give rides to others in the community.

Her children, now 20, 18 and 13, were able to get an education thanks to Rainbow scholarships. Because of this, the two older children are able to pay for their university tuition – studying accounting and computer engineering.

Even Jania, who is 36, is getting her education! She is in her third year of high school and hopes to become a nurse.

"I'm faithful that I am going to be able to get a career and move forward," she says. "You can get anything you want in life as long as you are determined and put your faith in God."

* * *

From Homeless to Homeowner

Maria Mendez was homeless, abandoned by her husband with seven children, when Rainbow Network made it possible for her to get her own home.

"I'm really grateful," she says. "I thank God, because thanks to Rainbow Network's support, I was able to obtain this house. Previously, my life was very tough. I was going house-to-house with my children, being a single mother. I lived in very sad situations until this project came in. Thank God I was chosen to be one of the beneficiaries. Now my life is quite different, thank God."

Rainbow also helped Maria send her children to high school, start a small business and get needed medical attention.

Today, Maria, who at 52 still has two children living at home, has paid off her house, something she never would have expected when Rainbow arrived in 1999. She was excited about the program and immediately volunteered to serve on various committees, often serving in leadership roles. Eight years ago, she was able to move into her own home. Today, she is the housing committee coordinator!

When her husband abandoned the family, she didn't know what she was going to do. "Imagine going house to house with seven children," she says. "But there is always someone the Lord sends you to help you. A lady let me use a small room. She would tell me, 'Don't get disappointed, God is going to give you a house.' And that is what happened."

"That is the reason I am so grateful. I always pray to God to help Rainbow Network because, thanks to them, many families are being benefitted."

* * *

Sent by God

Maria Valentina Hernandez Garcia owns her own home! The 67-year-old woman is proud to be able to say that today, but before Rainbow Network came into her community, she could not have imagined it.

"My house was really bad," she says of her life before Rainbow started the Cuajachillo 2 housing project. "It was about to fall apart, and my house didn't belong to me. It belonged to my stepson."

When Rainbow Network came into the community, she immediately saw that the organization was there to help. "I believed they would help us," she says. "I had hope that God actually sent them."

Maria was able to participate in micro loans in order to open a small pulperia in her home. "I sell rice, oil, snacks, tomatoes, chicken, a little bit of everything," she explains. With her children grown and married now, the store earns enough money to support her.

Her children benefitted from Rainbow scholarships so her daughter is now an accountant, her son an electrical engineer and her grandson a graphic designer.

"With faith in God, I believed they could become this," she says, but admits that if Rainbow had not come into her life, she would have had to leave her home to work in order to pay for their education.

Maria is a member of the housing committee and the loan bank, so she sees the needs in her community. "We could use more houses," she says. "There are people who need them."

* * *

Given a Chance

For Nubia Argentina Romero, having a house for her and her children was a goal that motivated her in many ways.

Nubia's is a "very sad story," she admits. She was a single mother working in sweat shops. She was depressed and overwhelmed, trying to support her three children while having to leave them to work. She lost a fourth baby who was born with malnutrition and leukemia. Her children's father didn't care about her or the children. "That's why I struggled alone," she says. "Since I didn't have anyone to support me, the only one that was there for me was Rainbow Network."

When Rainbow arrived, they were giving out applications for a housing project. "Nobody wanted me to apply for the house," Nubia remembers. "They were saying, 'You're too young and have no way of paying it back.' Since my life was a mess, I made a request."

The Rainbow staff knew what was going on in her life and took a chance on her. She worked hard, helping out the mason to build the houses. She sold vegetables on the street to buy milk for her children. "I survived until I was able to get my house and take a deep breath," she says.

Today, she is married to a hardworking man. She has another child with him and one on the way. "We both work hard for our family," she says. While her husband travels to work in factories, she stays home where she sells food out of her house and at the high school.

Her success as a business woman has meant that her older three daughters all went to high school without scholarships. "Since I couldn't make it, I want them to move forward and overcome poverty," she says.

Something to Think About

Read: Luke 11:9-13

1. What was the first prayer you learned as a child?
2. What was the funniest prayer you heard as a child?
3. Do you have a set time when you pray? Explain.
4. What items occupy most of your time in prayer?
5. Jesus said, "Ask and it will be given you..." Share an experience when you received.
6. What gift does Jesus conclude this lesson with?
7. Can you think of an example from this week's reading that shows answers to prayer in Nicaragua? Share.

Samuel Reyes may handle paperwork all day in his job with Rainbow Network, but it is the joy of seeing families succeed and communities prosper that makes his job so valuable. He says that Rainbow Network taught him the importance of giving to others.

The Rainbow Facts

At an average cost of $4,800 per house, Rainbow Network has spent more than $5.1 million dollars on its housing projects. Those loans are all paid back and reinvested into the ministry and the community.

CHAPTER FOUR

LEARNING TO SERVE

Samuel Reyes is responsible for managing all the money that comes into Rainbow Network in housing and loan payments. He began working for Rainbow 10 years ago as a translator for student and sponsor letters. He was impressed with the work Rainbow was doing and applied for full-time employment. With his English skills and a university education, he was able to work his way up to administrator out of the main office at Ciudad Sandino.

"We have been working on contracts, processes and structures," he says. "We now have a very strong structure for financial decisions. I am in charge of money, but I don't touch money at all. That is done on a local level."

Samuel goes through all the documents to make sure that government requirements are met. The Nicaraguan government goes through the records, looking over all payments and expenses. He is proud to report that Rainbow Network has passed muster, with no fines or changes. "That is unusual for NGOs," he says.

Having all the records available and welcoming inspectors to review documents is one of the reasons Rainbow works so well with government agencies. Samuel credits Keith Jaspers' business background.

"We do what we say," he insists. "If we say we will build 25 houses, they can go to the field and find the 25 houses. If we say we will give 700 scholarships, we do. If we say we give medical care, they can go to the community and see the changes. The government is checking. They want to make sure."

When the economy struggled after 2008, Rainbow Network did not stop doing what it said it would do.

"When we didn't have money, we would talk to the people about how to have clean water, etc.," Samuel says. "We were still there to give them everything we have. When we were going through a difficult time, they stayed with us."

Having built good relationships with other NGOs and governmental agencies allowed Rainbow to collaborate in order to continue all its services – education, feeding centers, medical care – even when finances were tight.

Since then, the organization has been doing better financially, Samuel says. "But we learned a lot from that situation." Money is stretched by finding the best products at the best prices and buying exactly what is needed.

It is this commitment to the people in all the communities served by Rainbow Network that has impressed Samuel, who remembers the poverty of his own childhood. He grew up living in a shack with 14 children and his parents. "I still remember starving for two days in a row, eating a tortilla with salt," he says. "We prayed morning, noon and night because we didn't have any food. Nobody helped us, but we believed God was with us because nobody died."

That is why he loves Rainbow Network and the work he does with the organization. "I've got to do something for people who lived like I did, children who are praying but no one is showing up," he says. "But Rainbow shows up."

He remembers being so hungry that he learned nothing in his first three years in school. "My stomach was thinking, not my mind," he says. "When I came to Rainbow Network, I saw the opportunity to give that something that nobody else gave to me or my family."

While Samuel sits behind a desk, working with checks and paperwork, he is committed to showing up for those starving children. "Here at Rainbow, we work with our heart," he says "We stay here because we love people."

Samuel speaks at churches in Nicaragua, teaching them about what Rainbow Network is doing, connecting it with the biblical story of the feeding of the 5,000. "When we don't know how to serve, we are like when Jesus was preaching to thousands of people and the disciples said, 'Let them go find food.' But Jesus said, 'We need to provide food for them.' That is our mission," Samuel explains. "That is what Rainbow is doing. People are donating so people can eat, get medical care, housing, a micro loan."

When Samuel tells those churches about what churches in the United States are doing for the people of Nicaragua, the message is resonating, he says. "They are impressed," he says. "They are starting to help. We are all poor, but everybody has a bag of rice or beans to give."

The word is also getting out throughout the country. "Churches are learning. Organizations are learning. The American Nicaraguan Foundation is coming here asking what we are doing," Samuel says.

But that is not enough for Samuel and his family. When the doors of the Rainbow Network office close on Friday afternoon for the weekend, he and his wife and four children head out into the community.

"We bring eggs from our chickens, used clothing," he says. "I learned this from Rainbow Network. In the past, I didn't think the way I'm thinking now. It is a blessing for me to learn and serve others. I came here to earn a salary and learned about serving."

Something to Think About

Read: Luke 9:46-48

1. Was there a time when you were honored for something you did? Share.
2. How does our society gauge greatness?
3. How does Jesus define greatness?
4. What characteristics of a little child make for greatness in us?
5. Who does the child in Jesus' example represent in our world?
6. How does receiving such a child mean receiving Christ?
7. In light of the above, who is greatest in Nicaragua today?
8. What story strikes you from Chapter 4?

Future homeowners help to construct the houses in a Rainbow Network housing project, and they pay for them through interest-free home loans.

CHAPTER FIVE

HOW IT WORKS

As in First World countries, home ownership and financing is the engine that drives the Rainbow Network economy.

Not only does home ownership raise the socio-economic status of individual home owners, it does the same for the community and the country. And it supports the many services provided through Rainbow Network.

As their stories demonstrate, families who are able to get a Rainbow house are also able to change their lives. The homes provide a stability and security that allows the family to focus on other aspects of their lives.

The homes can house businesses, from small stores called *pulperias* to family-based hammock or sewing factories. Dry and well-lighted, thanks to electricity that is brought into most Rainbow housing projects, students have a place to study and succeed in school. Floors that are made of concrete and easily kept clean, instead of the dirt floors the poor of rural Nicaragua most often have, mean that there are no parasites to battle or muddy ooze to contend with. With the wood-burning cook stoves outside of the living area, lungs can breathe free, keeping everyone healthier.

Rainbow housing projects turn into bustling little villages, with neighbors working together to improve everyone's life. With small local businesses and services, residents do not have to travel to find what they need. As each person succeeds financially, they are able to take advantage of the goods and services provided by their neighbors, and the entire community benefits.

Like any mortgage bank, Rainbow Network's housing committees determine if an applicant for a home is a good financial risk. The committee is made up of community leaders who are committed to making the project succeed. As in the Habitat for Humanity program, once a family is approved for a Rainbow home, they are required to contribute labor and learn how to be responsible homeowners. Each family provides the "sweat equity" needed to build the entire housing project. Often, friends and relatives will help the family meet those

35

requirements, which makes this a true community project. The families will not know which of the houses will be their home until the dedication ceremony, so they work equally as hard on each house.

All construction is supervised by a Rainbow Network staff foreman, and supporting churches often send teams of volunteers to help with some of the basic labor.

The houses are identical, with an average of 25 built in each project. The 320-square-foot houses are made up of 540 concrete blocks, secured with rebar to keep the house standing when the inevitable earthquakes strike. In fact, not a single Rainbow house has been damaged or destroyed in any earthquakes, despite other buildings suffering much damage!

Besides creating rooms inside the home, families often build covered, open-air rooms off the house to provide more space for family activities. And the covered, concrete front porch gives the family a shaded and breezy spot to sit. The kitchens, built outside of the house, include a wood-burning stove for cooking and many times will have a sink and even a makeshift shower, depending on the family's needs and resources. The shiny metal outhouses at the back of each property are an important part of the health and safety of all Rainbow communities.

In this warm, tropical climate, it only takes a few months for each of the houses to bloom with vegetation. Families plant flowers to celebrate the beauty of this country and gardens to keep their tables full of fresh produce. Houses and fences are painted in colorful hues, and each house takes on the personality of the family inside.

Each of those families has also taken on an important responsibility, to pay back the $4,800 it takes to build their home. That is done through 20- to 25-year no-interest Rainbow Network loans, reflecting the program's roots in Habitat for Humanity. All homeowners take part in Rainbow Network's micro-loan program, which creates more opportunities for security and helps to maintain the nearly 100 percent repayment rate on the $17-per-month mortgages. The pride and empowerment built through this model transfers into responsibility and lifelong benefits for homeowners and their children.

Churches and other groups across the United States have stepped up to support the Rainbow housing projects. When a church donates the money to build a house, that money does much more than underwrite construction. It provides a long-term income that will ensure that Rainbow Network can continue to serve that community and many more communities throughout rural Nicaragua. The mortgage payments made by recipient families go back into the ministry, so these families are not only paying for their home, they are paying toward the health of their entire community. They are contributing to the economy of their community and their country.

This is not unlike the story of Jesus feeding the multitudes with just a few fish and loaves of bread. God's love and bounty is made available to so many people when those who have a few fish – or dollars – step up.

* * *

Success in Los Pinos

The people of La Grecia are still waiting for those same opportunities. They continue to live in homes made of sticks and black plastic sheeting, with dirt floors that turn to mud when it rains. The poverty is heartbreaking and the needs are many. Rainbow Network has been working toward finding available land and support for a housing project, so these people have hope. Like other similar communities, however, they are still waiting for a dry, safe and secure home to help them begin to build their lives.

They have only to look at the changes that have come to the nearby community of Los Pinos. Rainbow Network has been working with Los Pinos since establishing the San Ramon Network in 2002, when economic and political unrest left the region without work or assistance. With no jobs and no way to feed their families, area residents took to the streets to strike for jobs, food and medicine.

That is when Rainbow Network arrived, says Angela Davila, who has served as community coordinator since then. A natural leader, Angela was already serving the community in other ways. She understands her position must be underscored by hard work and genuine care for her neighbors.

Angela has organized her neighbors to succeed by working closely with Rainbow Network. Families who had been living in the same kind of housing found in La Grecia now own their own homes through Rainbow Network, and many others have found ways to support their families through micro loans. With regular medical services available and education attainable, Los Pinos has blossomed, and residents are looking to the future.

"Our dreams for our youth is to have a baseball field," says Angela. "That is what our youth are clamoring for."

As coordinator, Angela leads the twice-a-year community meetings in Los Pinos. Everyone who can get there attends the meetings, filling the community center, while others gather around the doors and windows to hear what is being said.

Before starting the meeting, someone says a prayer. These people know that, while they work hard and Rainbow Network contributes important resources, it is God who provides. The successes of Los Pinos are blessings from God and answers to prayers.

Next, Angela introduces her committee members – representing housing, education, scholarships, micro loans, family care and nutrition. Angela reports that 23 people have used the doctor, including for ultrasounds, and the dentist for extractions, since the last meeting. The community now has 16 scholarship students, she says.

"Rainbow Network is the only way we could have accomplished this," she says.

But success doesn't mean Los Pinos is without problems. People express their concerns that the cistern is getting low on water. Another worries that neighbors who do not keep their property clean and free of standing water could be attracting mosquitoes, which carry dengue fever and the zika virus. Rainbow staff is on hand to offer suggestions and solutions, and soon the conversation moves from concerns to celebrations.

None of the children of Los Pinos has been held back in school this year, Angela reports as those gathered smile and nod in delight at the news.

"We thank Rainbow Network and pray for them every day," one woman in the crowd says.

Something to Think About

Read: Matthew 25:31-46

1. How was your house heated / cooled as a child?
2. When were you in need, and someone helped you? Explain. (i.e. Hungry... Thirsty... Stranger... In need of Shelter... Sick... Imprisoned...).
3. When did you share with someone with no reason to expect something in return?
4. How did you feel after #1 and/or #2 above?
5. Why is it important to give to "the least of these?"
6. How does that tie in with what it means to be a Christian?
7. Was Jesus serious when He tied giving to the poor with one's salvation? Explain.
8. What inspired you most concerning the housing projects in Nicaragua?

Supporters who travel to Nicaragua with Rainbow Network have an opportunity to meet community residents like these two industrious young men.

CHAPTER SIX

HOW YOU CAN HELP

The welfare of Los Pinos is a special concern to the members of Woods Chapel United Methodist Church in Lees Summit, Missouri. That church has taken on this little community as its neighbor, providing scholarships for high school students, raising money for housing projects and helping support special medical needs. But this church family has taken an extra step to truly become neighbors with the people of Los Pinos.

Twice a year, a group from the church visits Los Pinos, visiting each of the residents to take a "census" and make personal connections. They know families by name and ask about how things have been going since the previous visit. The community plans welcome events where church members can connect with their scholarship students.

Woods Chapel also provided the financing for the housing project at La Corona, which is also in the San Ramon Network, and they have made inroads in the isolated community of Los Encuentros in the Ciudad Dario Network, only recently connected by a road. Here, for generations, the residents have earned a living tanning cow hides for leather workers who make beautiful saddles, belts and other leather goods. The hides are cleaned in the creek that runs through the community, then laid on the rock outcrops to dry. Next, they are dyed with cacao beans.

There are no cars or trucks in Los Encuentros, and they still do not have electricity. Horses are the main mode of transportation, and the children ride with ease and fast! They have been isolated for so long that the people of Los Encuentros have had little communication outside of the small community, but now the children are able to go to school and at least one family will make their home down the road at a new Rainbow Network housing project in La Quesera.

Bill and Pam Carpenter are members of Woods Chapel and have embraced the church's work with Rainbow Network. They visit regularly, and Bill keeps a blog where he and other church members share their experiences. Here are some excerpts written by Stacy Scott from a February 2016 trip that included the dedication at La Corona:

"*Just a short flight, but a whole world away, Nicaragua tries to survive. Not in the daily grind most of us in the states know, but to actually make it to tomorrow. One of the poorest countries in this hemisphere, poverty wreaks havoc throughout their communities. Many parents don't know where their children's next meal will come from (or even if there will be a next meal).*

"*This is my third year traveling to the villages of Nicaragua, and each year I come hoping to help any way that I can. But in truth, each year, we help each other. This community has become family. This community reminds me what we are missing. Life is so precious yet we forget to take time to really appreciate it. They don't forget that here. That is the very core of what keeps them going every day.*

"*Today … today, we saw beds. How amazing is that? Something we take for granted every day, but such a luxury for the people of Los Pinos. We saw beds today. I want to say that again. We saw beds today! Three years ago, we saw wood planks with blankets and mud floors.*

"*We can go to the corner store or local Walmart and get dinner or anything we need, anytime of day – 24 hours a day. Here, they wait until they get off work, take a long bus ride in to town to get supplies they need, and then ride a long bus ride back home … and that is an adventure, I can attest. And still, most of these people don't ever see the outside of their tiny little village. They don't ever get to venture to the big cities or to normal stores. They don't have normal transportation or means to go beyond the couple-mile road that runs up and down the villages that lie nearby. Their entire world consists of family and friends within a 10-mile radius of where they live. Can you imagine? The furthest thing you ever get to see is within 100 blocks of your home?*

"*Today I got to play tag with a group of girls. They accepted us as their own and were grateful just to be loved. These girls have stolen my heart every time I visit. I come back each year just to see their smiles. They remind me what life is all about. It's not about fancy things or what we can buy. It's about love … and these kids love with their whole hearts. These kids are our future and we have the opportunity to make it better. They are grateful despite their circumstances. To come here, you wouldn't know that they have health issues or concerns.*

"*So, who is better off? That is a tough one. We are blessed in so many ways, but so are they. Today they welcomed us as family. They felt like family. No one is better than another. We have the opportunity to help them live and they have the opportunity to help us know how to love living. How cool is that?*

"*Sitting staring at the bright starlit sky tonight, tears and all, I couldn't help but thank God for the amazing gift he allowed these amazing friends to bring in to my life. They are truly blessed and I am truly blessed for knowing them. God has given us the means to help each other, thousands of miles apart, all children blessed by His grace.*

"Our job is not yet done. They are still dying of smoke inhalation and malnutrition, yet still so thankful to just be alive. They praise for everything, they praise just for waking up. They get to wake up every day to an amazing view, to an amazing family, to a community full of friends and loved ones. They love their life, they love waking up, they love just being. We have helped so many, but there are still many more… lovingly, patiently, hopefully and prayerfully waiting for us to come."

"God, guide my heart, my arms I hold wide open. Lord show me, guide me, I am yours."

Not every church that partners with Rainbow Network has the same level of involvement. Some are only able to provide financial assistance. While many supporters are able to visit Nicaragua at least once, that is not the only way to connect.

For example, one year the youth at Schweitzer United Methodist in Springfield, Missouri, built a replica of the typical mud and stick house many Nicaraguan families live in. They constructed it outside the church and used it as a teaching tool and a way to raise awareness and money for Rainbow Network

On a recent Pentecost Sunday, St. Peter's Evangelical United Church of Christ in Billings, Missouri, invited Rainbow's Development Director Megan Munzlinger to speak about the work being done in Nicaragua. The congregation donated money and took home information as several members began discussing a possible mission trip in the future.

The Rev. Mel Miller, a retired Methodist pastor, has been a Rainbow Network supporter for years, although he has never been able to visit Nicaragua. Working with his church, Community Christian Church in Springfield, the nonagenarian collects shoes all year to send down to Nicaragua. One year, he and his church collected more than 2,250 pairs.

Mark and Dorothy Harsen of Springfield have been supporters since 2003 after taking a mission trip there with their church. On that trip, Mark helped to build one of the Rainbow houses. He tells the story of how that experience changed his life.

As he began working hard in the hot sun, one Nicaraguan man began to take an interest in him, demonstrating with gestures since neither spoke the other's language that he should drink more water and find some shade. As Mark and the others prepared to leave, the man told him through an interpreter that he would pray for him every day.

"I said, 'No, I will pray for you. You shouldn't have to pray for me. I come from the land of plenty. I have a house and a car and plenty of food.' He shook his head at me and said, 'I will pray for you every day. How can you see God clearly through all those things?' That changed my life."

Some churches have raised enough money for entire housing projects, while others may raise funds for one or two houses. Groups of churches working together have supported housing projects, while individual donors have helped to pay for various pieces of a project such as the land or water system.

Various groups within Cross International have funded projects although the donors may never actually visit Nicaragua.

But it is those visits, when visitors see the stick and plastic homes so many poor Nicaraguans call home, that have the most impact. That is the sight that brings people to tears. Such a tangible example of extreme poverty has opened people's hearts to Nicaragua and Rainbow Network. And when hearts are opened, the Spirit works there.

Something to Think About

Read: Matthew 15:32-39

1. What is your favorite family meal?
2. Is there a time when you wondered where the next meal would come from? Explain.
3. Why did Jesus feed the multitude according to the Lesson for today?
4. When have you been moved with compassion to give? How did it feel?
5. Where did the food come from with which the multitude was fed?
6. When have you given a little, and seen it magnified by God? Explain.
7. If Jesus were in the flesh again, where would He go to minister to hungry people?
8. How is He "in the flesh" today? (See I Corinthians 12:27)

Healthcare

Heal the sick, raise the dead, cleanse lepers, cast out demons.

Matthew 10:8

Sarah Janellis is just one example of the medical "miracles" that happen when Rainbow Network joins with a community. Thanks to surgeries provided through the Special Medical Needs program, Sarah can walk.

CHAPTER SEVEN

THE LAME SHALL WALK

Despite the uneven terrain and her unsteady gait, Sarah Jannellis happily leads her visitors down the rutted path to the garden she tends for her family. The 17-year-old girl points out the homes of her grandmothers and her uncle and tempts her visitors with mangos from a tree outside her home.

Sarah was born with shortened tendons that prevented her from straightening her legs and learning to walk until Rainbow Network doctors diagnosed her problem and Rainbow supporters raised the money needed for surgery. She was only a child at the time, but Sarah's tenacity and spunk have seen her through many challenges.

Today, she is a teenager with big plans for her future thanks to the support she, her family and her village of Cuajachillo have received from Rainbow Network. She is finishing high school and plans to study English. Talking to her guests, she brags with certainty, "Next time, I will be talking to you directly. I won't need a translator."

Sarah comes by her confidence naturally. Her great-grandfather, Domingo, was an important leader in the Cuajachillo community when Keith Jaspers arrived to offer the services of Rainbow Network. Keith remembers that until Domingo stepped up, he had little success explaining the program and getting people to participate. But Domingo understood and knew that with the help of Rainbow Network, Cuajachillo could prosper.

At an anniversary celebration at Ciudad Sandino, where the network office is located, Sarah's grandmother Angela Mercado was honored on behalf of her late father as a pioneer for Cuajachillo. Angela is now the community organizer, taking over the family tradition of leading her community. With her determination and spirit, Sarah is destined to do the same some day.

But when Sarah was just a child, her future did not look as bright. Her mother, Esther Sanchez, remembers that she took Sarah to the children's hospital in Managua because the girl still could not stand up straight to walk. The doctors there told her there was nothing to be done but to let her "learn how to walk, one way or the other."

47

Then a Rainbow doctor arrived in the community. Dr. Gabriel Morella told her that Rainbow could help. He took X-rays and did some tests and determined that surgery was the answer. The surgery would cost $1,000, so Sarah was listed as one of the special medical needs, and Rainbow supporters were asked to help raise the money. They came through, and Sarah went to the hospital, where the tendons from her ankle to her hip were straightened.

Sarah wasted no time learning to walk, but another surgery is needed now that she has grown. Her mother worries that something could go wrong, but Sarah is determined that she will someday get the second surgery. She is now able to walk, but her gait is unsteady and slow. She worries that it could prevent her from getting a good job someday. It does prevent her from going to school some days during the rainy season when the roads are too muddy and slippery for her to safely walk, but she perseveres, determined to complete her high school and go on to college someday.

Even though she was only 6 years old when she had the surgery, she remembers well the emotional and physical pain. Before the surgery, she had to crawl or wear flip flops on her hands to get around. She went to school, but she was bullied because of her disability, so she didn't want to go outside. Unlike today, she was afraid and withdrawn.

'I remember perfectly," she says through a translator. "There are things I will never forget. I felt as though I didn't exist on the planet, as if I wasn't important to anybody. The very first time I got to the school, they looked at me very weirdly, and I suffered bullying. Now, I am stronger every day. Now, if someone laughs at me, I say, 'Thank you. You are making me stronger.'"

Learning to walk was difficult. She came home from the hospital with casts on her legs and a metal bar between her feet. She tried to stand up even with the casts on. She fell down, but that didn't stop her. Unwilling to wait any longer, she and her brothers took the cast off rather than going back to the hospital.

She started walking with small steps after about a month, falling down but getting back up.

"It was kind of weird at the very beginning," she says. "I spent six years without walking. It was nice."

Her determination has never waned. The same effort she puts into walking is evident in her education and her work at home. "I will continue to struggle, become more eager, and I will succeed," she says.

A typical teenager, she also loves music. Her favorite band is One Direction.

She is quick with a joke, especially a sarcastic one, but she hopes someday to start an organization that will help children. "They don't need to have the same problems I have, but I think my experience will help me do that," she says.

In the meantime, she has other big plans. First, she will finish high school and go on to college, like two of her older sisters. She also hopes to participate in Rainbow's micro loan program, using her talent making piñatas to help support her family.

Then she would like to write her autobiography, "The Story of My Life." Her inspiration was looking through the correspondence with her scholarship sponsor. "It made me think about writing my story, as a memory," she says.

Her great-grandfather Domingo would be proud of his sassy and self-confident great-granddaughter Sarah. She is an example of determination and grit.

Her journey has also given her beautiful insight.

While pointing out the road that runs up to her family's property, she jokes that her visitors could walk back to Ciudad Sandino. But the way is too long, one visitor objects. She smiles slightly and shakes her head.

"If you walk with your friends, you don't even notice the distance."

* * *

Inspiration in a First Step

Joiner Ramon Perez Urtado took his first steps at eight years old. Six months later, the tiny boy walks across the room slowly and with determination, but without assistance. He is even able to go outside and play with friends.

Four years earlier, Joiner was a mystery, kept hidden from sight because of a cleft palate and club feet. When Rainbow representatives finally learned about Joiner they stepped in immediately. Too heavy for his mother to carry any longer, the only way Joiner was going to go anywhere was if he had surgery to correct his condition and therapy to learn to walk.

"I have to admit it, we were afraid to have the surgery," says his mother, Darling Urtado. "But then Dr. Candido started talking to us and told us that it's not fair to leave your child like that. He came to our house and let us know that they had someone to finance it and had the help. He convinced us to have the surgery."

The cost to repair both his cleft palate and club feet was too much for Joiner's family. His father, Bonifacio Perez, works in the field about four months of the year making barely enough money to feed his family. Although they now live in a Rainbow house, at that time they were forced to live with a friend.

A plea for this special medical case brought in a donation from a supporter. Luke Nixon of Springfield agreed to put up enough money to pay for the surgeries and the needed physical therapy.

In 2013, Rainbow worked with another NGO that performed Joiner's first surgery to correct his cleft palate. Finally able to eat and breathe normally, the little boy soon recovered, but he still could not walk. On June 25, 2014, Joiner and his mother left their home and traveled for over four hours to the city of Leon where Rainbow Network helped set up the process to correct his club feet.

After five weeks in casts to straighten his legs, Joiner finally had surgery on both his legs on July 31, 2014. He wears splints to stretch his ankles and special orthopedic shoes, provided by his Rainbow sponsor, to help him walk.

In January of 2015, Joiner experienced a true miracle. He took his first step!

Soon, at age 8, he walked into school for the first time in his life. He started attending a Rainbow Network primary school and now has the opportunity to earn an education and follow his dream of becoming a teacher – or maybe a mechanic. After years of being hidden, alone and friendless, Joiner now is able to play with other children and even has a special friend, Oliver. They talk, play marbles and play a little soccer.

Joiner has inspired so many people with his determination, his wide smile and his warm heart. Megan Munzlinger keeps a picture of the little boy on her desk to lift her heart when she is down and to remind her of the miracles God performs through Rainbow Network. She loves to tell the story of Joiner but never fails to tear up in the telling.

Dr. Candido sees tragic cases and miraculous recoveries every day in his work through Rainbow Network, but he always mentions Joiner as an inspiration. So do the other doctors and staff in Nicaragua.

* * *

As Long as the Lord Provides

Harvin Sotela Cruz hopes that he can be an inspiration to Joiner. Harvin was born with Distal Arthrogyposis Syndrome, a muscular-skeletal condition that causes his joints to continually contract. He seemed normal at birth, but by the age of four, the disease left him unable to walk or use his hands.

The impact of Harvin's condition was hard on his mother, Jacinta Sotelo. A single mom, she had little money or resources, including fresh water. She worked long hours selling her homemade tamales to provide for her two children, but as Harvin grew, his needs increased, too. Doctors had told her there was nothing that could be done for her son until he was at least 15 years old.

When Rainbow Network arrived in their small village in the San Ramon region, the staff heard about Harvin. Assessing his condition, the Rainbow doctors were able to get him the necessary treatments, including more than 20 surgeries, specialty physicians and therapy.

The family was able to move into a Rainbow house, with electricity and access to fresh water, in the community of Hilapo 2, which is supported by National Avenue Christian Church in Springfield, Missouri, through Rainbow Network's Village Sponsorship Program. Samaritan's Purse provided funds initially, and then Rainbow supporters were able to raise the money needed to complete Harvin's medical care.

Harvin did not let them down. He was determined to walk. "I started walking even though my legs still had casts," he says. "I still tried. It wasn't hard because I was determined to do it."

He has met Joiner. "He is struggling like I did," he says. "I can encourage him."

At 16, Harvin is in his second year of high school, attending on a Rainbow scholarship and hopes to continue his education at the university. Despite being held back by his illness, Harvin is intelligent and quickly caught up.

Although he continues to have pain and faces many more surgeries, he loves to play sports. He is a center fielder in baseball and plays defense in soccer.

His mother calls her son's achievements "a triumph of life," made possible by God through Rainbow Network. Jacinta has also triumphed. She continues to sell her tamales, which Harvin calls the "best in town," to support her sons and pay for her home. She paid off a micro loan and sometimes struggles financially, but she is as determined as Harvin to succeed.

"As long as the Lord provides me with the strength to keep on working, I will make it," she said.

Something to Think About

Read: Acts 3:1-10

1. If you had to beg to live – what would your day look like?
2. What did the lame man ask of Peter and John?
3. What did Peter say to him?
4. What did Peter do for him in the name of Jesus Christ?
5. Have you ever been wondrously healed? Explain.
6. Can you name one person who was healed because of Rainbow Network?

When she was just a baby, cataracts caused by malnutrition were robbing Iris Karina Merlo Menendez of her vision. A donation from a U.S. church group made it possible for Iris to have surgery, and today she is the mother of a healthy, bright-eyed baby girl.

CHAPTER EIGHT

THE BLIND SHALL SEE

Sarah, Joiner and Harvin are just a few of hundreds, even thousands, of children and adults who have been given the gift of medical care through Rainbow Network. It is one of the most important parts of the Rainbow program.

Using the examples of Jesus Christ as his guide, Keith Jaspers knew that providing safe housing for people was not enough. Through Jesus, the lame walked, the blind were given sight and the deaf could hear. Rainbow Network was called to do the same.

Sarah, Joiner and Harvin now walk.

Iris Karina Merlo Menendez now sees.

Iris Karina was a beautiful, dark-eyed baby, but malnutrition left those big, brown eyes covered by blinding cataracts. As she grew, her vision got worse, making school and socializing difficult for the youngster.

Then Rainbow Network arrived in the Los Fierros community in El Crucero, where Keith Jaspers first encountered the shy girl clutching her mother's leg. Rainbow doctors examined the girl, discovering the problem and proposing a solution. They told her parents, Ilda Menendez and Donaldo Merlo, that an operation would give Iris Karina, the youngest of their five children, her sight. But the cataract surgery would cost $1,000. The government doctors would not do the surgery for free, and the family had no way of raising that kind of money.

It happened that National Avenue Christian Church in Springfield, Missouri had sent a team down to Nicaragua to learn more about Rainbow Network, which the church had begun supporting. Iris Karina and her parents were at the office when the team arrived. When they learned that Rainbow had not yet been able to raise the full amount for the girl's surgery, the visitors reached into their own pockets and came up with the money needed.

A year later, the pastor of the church was in the same office when the family arrived for a meeting. His blue eyes lit up when he saw Iris Karina, her large brown eyes wide as she looked around the room.

That is the kind of miracle that Rainbow Network makes possible.

Today, Iris Karina is a young wife and mother. Her baby girl, Ainara, is a healthy, fat-cheeked little one with the same beautiful, big, brown eyes. But hers are clear and her vision true. Grandma and Grandpa obviously love Ainara, who smiles for Grandpa as he makes faces at her while Grandma holds her.

"We were really desperate," says Donaldo of those many years ago when Iris Karina was a baby. "We didn't know what to do. Thank God for Rainbow Network."

"I thank God to have Rainbow Network in my life," says Iris Karina, at 18. "If not for Rainbow Network I would not see at all now. Thanks to them, I have the life I have today. ... I also thank the people of the United States who gave money for my operation."

"Rainbow Network was the blessing that God gave to my family," adds Ilda.

That blessing did not end with Iris Karina's surgery. In addition to helping with continued medical care and glasses for the girl, as well as needed nutrition, Rainbow supporters provided scholarships for Iris Karina and her brothers. One brother got a scholarship to attend college, where he earned a degree in business administration. Iris Karina would love to study English and psychology.

For now, she lives with her parents, but she and her husband will soon move into a new wooden house nearby built by Roof For My Country, an organization run by a group of private companies in Nicaragua. Because of Rainbow Network's reputation, the group went to Rainbow to ask about where there was a need. Roof For My Country built six homes in Los Fierros, including Iris Karina's.

Ilda and Donaldo are farmers, raising corn, beans, wheat and yucca. The drought and a plague on the beans has been hard on them, but Donaldo expects to harvest about 40 100-pound bags – enough to feed the family and sell some at the market.

* * *

They live in a simple wooden house with a dirt floor, but it is tidy and solid. In fact, the dirt floor and even the hard dirt around the house are swept clean.

Ilda is president of the community, and Donaldo helps in activities such as the feeding center, where he carries water six kilometers in his ox cart. Iris Karina is on the health committee.

For the Merlo family, the biggest miracle has been Iris Karina's eyesight, but they point out that the impact on their community has also been great. "A lot of families are able to get an education," says Ilda. "And a lot of children with malnutrition get healthy."

"It is good help for the poor people," adds Donaldo, "like us."

*   *   *

Seeing the Future

Edelma Roa Picon is a beautiful young mother. She stays home with her children while her husband works as an air conditioning technician. In their village of San Isidro, Nagarote, Edelma is a community leader, in charge of the feeding center and the Rainbow school in the afternoon.

It is hard to imagine the insecure girl Edelma used to be.

At two years old, Edelma lost her right eye to a tumor. Doctors tried to save her eye, but ultimately had to remove it, leaving her face disfigured. She struggled with her self-esteem as the other children made fun of her.

"When I was in primary school, it was really tough," she says. "But in high school, it was different. That's when Rainbow Network showed up."

She turned to "Senor Keith," asking him if there was anything that could be done. Rainbow arranged to have the teenager looked at by an ophthalmologist, who said she needed plastic surgery to repair the eye socket and cheekbone before a prosthetic eye could be inserted.

Rainbow Network supporters raised the funds needed for the surgery – $500, much more than her family could ever afford to pay – and on her 15th birthday, Edelma's life was changed.

"Before, I was really embarrassed and ashamed," she recalls, acknowledging that as a young teen her appearance was of great importance. "After the surgery, I wasn't embarrassed at all. I feel like I am like any other normal person. I don't have any negative complex."

Edelma went on to complete high school through a Rainbow scholarship, tutoring the younger children at the Rainbow school, and immediately becoming a leader in the community.

Every three years, she must return to get a new glass eye. Her most recent surgery was possible through the support of Source Youth

Ministry at Wesley United Methodist Church in Springfield, Missouri, a regular Rainbow supporter.

She is now focused on her children. Her 10-year-old son is bright and doing well in school, while her 2-year-old daughter is still at home. But Edelma has plans for them both. "I will send them to high school," she says with confidence.

Edelma "sees" a future for her and her children, thanks to Rainbow Network and its supporters.

Something to Think About

Read: John 9:1-11

1. Have you ever played a game where you were blindfolded?
2. What was it like not to be able to see?
3. Have you known personally someone who could not see?
4. How did they cope?
5. Can you name a person from this chapter who was healed?
6. What would it be like to be able to announce: "Once I was blind, but now I see!"?

Dr. Candido Calderius Rios uses a portable ultrasound machine to see the position of a woman's unborn baby. Dr. Candido, as he is known, joined the Rainbow Network staff in 2007 and has found faith and fulfilment in his work.

CHAPTER NINE

A Good Doctor

For many people in Rainbow Network communities, the Rainbow doctors provided the first medical care available. It became apparent early in Rainbow's history that a permanent medical staff would be necessary, but finding good doctors who were willing to do this hard work was a challenge.

When Candido Calderius Rios joined the Rainbow Network staff in 2002, it didn't take long to recognize that he was just what the doctor ordered – a good doctor! Today, he is the medical supervisor for the entire program, but everyone in the small communities in each of the seven networks knows him. He has touched so many lives.

One of his specialties now is the ultrasound. Although that technology may be commonplace in the United States, it is rare in these poor, rural communities of Nicaragua. Dr. Candido traveled to Wisconsin to learn to use the machine, and now he and his portable ultrasound equipment are common and welcome sights in the Rainbow Network communities.

A group of doctors from Gundersen Lutheran Medical Center in La Crosse, Wisconsin, traveled to Nicaragua on a mission trip and decided that Dr. Candido needed to do ultrasounds there. So they donated the portable machine and gave him the training he needed to use it. He has found tumors and other medical issues with his machine, but his most common patient is a pregnant woman excited to see her growing baby on the screen and to be reassured that the baby is healthy. Iris Karina was one of those women when she was pregnant with Ainara!

At a clinic in El Carmen, eight pregnant women, many with young children clinging to their legs, sit under the shade of a covered porch, waiting their turn to get their ultrasound done in a home donated to use for the clinic.

Inside, there is room for a small bed and the table where the amazing machine sits. Each woman lies down as Candido slides the probe over the mother's belly to send the sound waves to the computer. He looks at the results to see if the pregnancy is going as expected, to be sure the heart is working and, especially in the case of late term pregnancies, to

61

make sure the umbilical cord is not wrapped around the baby's neck. He can then send the report to the hospital where the women will deliver the babies.

Through it all, Candido quietly explains what he is doing and seeing and answers any questions.

"This is the heart!" he exclaims to one women who is due in about two weeks. "And there's the head."

Another woman is younger and only 22 weeks along. "Look at this," Candido tells her. "It's a baby!" He tells her that the baby is fine and now all she has to do is wait.

"I love this machine and my yacht," he jokes. "This is my baby! My portable machine."

Nearly every Rainbow community has stories about Dr. Candido, about lives he saved and lives he changed. In 2003, when Rainbow began the La Dalia project, he was the first physician most of the residents had ever seen. They lined up for hours along the hillside waiting to step into his makeshift office and told him about their ailments.

Over the years, the people have grown to love Candido, and he has grown to love them. He is especially attached to those patients with special needs and is always grateful when supporters in the United States step up to meet those needs.

Born and raised in Cuba, where he studied medicine, he came to Nicaragua in 1986 after the revolution. Cuba sent many doctors, teachers, and other specialists to help the fledgling Sandinista government. Candido fell in love with the country – and fell in love, marrying a Nicaraguan wife and ultimately had three children.

About a half dozen years after joining Rainbow Network, something miraculous also happened to Candido. He became a Christian! Born right after Cuba's revolution in 1959, Candido was not taught about religion at all. But in Nicaragua, even communism couldn't wipe out the people's faith, and Rainbow Network is unashamed of its Christian foundation.

Candido and his family began to seek a relationship with God, "because we are clear that he is our savior," he says. For a child of the Cuban revolution, it took time and effort to understand.

"The first time I touched a Bible was in Rainbow Network," he says. But now the family worships regularly at a church, and Candido declares that he is happy and calls himself a "soldier for Christ."

Something to Think About

Read: Mark 5:21-42

1. When you were a child what vaccinations do you remember getting? Describe.
2. With a multitude around Jesus, the desperate woman muscles her way through the crowd, and touches His garment. With so many jostling Him, why did He notice?
3. Where do you see the Lord's compassion for this woman?
4. What are some of the feelings a sick person has when there is no help?
5. Have you ever been in a helpless situation? Explain.
6. How does it make you feel when you read of the multitudes of persons Rainbow Network has helped?
7. What can you do to help expand this ministry?

Dr. Veronica Chavarria is one of ten Rainbow Network doctors who regularly hold medical clinics in each of the more than 140 Rainbow Network communities. Dr. Veronica's smile puts children and adults at ease, and the medical care she gives them is an essential part of creating healthy communities.

CHAPTER TEN

HOW IT WORKS

There are ten doctors and one dentist on the Rainbow Network staff. Each makes regular rounds to all of the more than 140 Rainbow communities, holding clinics in community buildings, schools or private homes, so people are able to get consistent care and follow-up.

Because of that, doctors at Rainbow communities rarely see malnutrition-related conditions any longer. Now, most of the clinics bring families with nothing more than colds and rashes, aches and pains. Dr. Veronica Chavarria saw several of those cases during a clinic in El Carmen.

The clinic is held in the community center, with sheets hung on a clothes line to separate the "doctor's office" from the "waiting room." Community volunteers handle the medical records, as mothers bounce fussy babies on their knees and call out to children who have wriggled free and wandered off to find a playmate.

Patients are asked to pay a minimal fee for their care, although no one is turned away if they are unable to pay. The fees not only help to support the medical program, they also give each family a sense of empowerment, knowing that they are not getting charity.

Dr. Veronica invites her patients in and quickly puts them at ease with her easy laugh and gentle spirit. One mother brings in her two young children. The 3-year-old boy has had a fever and a cough, but Dr. Veronica determines he has no infection and hands his mother a bottle of acetaminophen and vitamins donated by the Vitamin Angels. The 6-year-old girl is there for a follow-up visit after having an eye infection.

Clinics such as these happen every day throughout the Rainbow communities. Doctors from the United States have worked with Rainbow's doctors over the years, often learning as much as the Nicaraguan doctors do from them.

Sometimes miracles happen, such as the amazing zinc oxide cure!

For years, women with open leg ulcers came to the clinics. They had been untreated for years, and many were so bad the women could no longer walk. One year, Dr. Robert Carolla, who later served as president of the Rainbow Network Board of Directors, and Dr. Tom Froehlich, both oncologists, joined Keith Jaspers on a trip to Nicaragua. While they were there, the Rainbow doctors brought in several of these women to see the U.S. doctors.

No one knew how to treat the problem, which brought such pain that amputation was being considered. Dr. Carolla and Dr. Froehlich both insisted that the condition was treatable – but neither of them remembered how. Dr. Froehlich asked the doctors not to do any amputations but to give him some time to make a few phone calls after he returned home.

A few days later, Dr. Froehlich called Keith. The remedy was simple zinc oxide. Rainbow workers ran out to Kmart and bought a case of the small tubes, sending them to Nicaragua with instructions to apply the cream on the open ulcers three to four times a day. After a few weeks, all were healed!

Victoria Castro was one of those women. Today, at 71, the tiny woman walks easily and is happy to lift her right leg up on a chair to show off the small scar left from the terrible ulcer. She explains that a thorn got in her leg, which swelled up and turned purple. "It happened in January," she recalls. "By the end of the month, it was badly swollen. That lasted for years, until they were able to give me the treatment. It was a small vial. It looked like spaghetti."

Victoria's grown children were frantic as their mother's leg got worse and worse until she could no longer walk and was in constant pain. They heard that some Rainbow Network folks would be passing by on a road miles from her home, so they carried her in a plastic chair all the way to the road and waited until the pickup truck carrying the two doctors was in sight. Then they flagged them down and begged for help for their mother.

The staff didn't hesitate. Victoria was soon on her way to a Rainbow doctor and the zinc oxide treatment she needed to recover. Later, she would undergo physical therapy to regain her strength and ability to walk.

"I was happy because I was able to do anything at home without the crutches or a cane," Victoria says, punctuating her words with frequent burst of joyful laughter. "I am happy for all the help that I got."

* * *

Responding to Starvation

While some medical miracles come in small tubes of zinc oxide, others require months of effort. That was the case in 2000 when reports out of the mountainous coffee plantation region of Matagalpa were that a lot of people were dying due to starvation. Teams of Rainbow folks went to investigate.

The teams reported that about a dozen communities in the San Ramon area were desperate, with some communities reporting 15-20 deaths a month. With coffee prices depressed, work at the plantations became scarce, and people who had lived on the shuttered plantations for generations were now jobless and homeless. The adult literacy rate was only about 10 percent, so there were few other job opportunities for these people. Families were forced to steal and eat green plantains, boiled over an open fire. Children were drinking water from ditches.

Rainbow's response was in stages. After identifying the most needy families, truckloads of rice and beans, cooking oil and fruit were sent to each of the communities where the food was distributed to the starving families. To avoid riots, each family was given a ticket and the truck stopped at several scheduled locations where the food was passed out to hundreds of people who had been waiting anxiously.

At the same time, a half dozen physicians were sent with large quantities of basic medicines. They set up temporary clinics along the sides of roads where the sick and dying waited patiently in long lines. Dr. Candido recalls the lines trailing down the mountainside; so long he could not see the end.

This program of food distribution and medical care was repeated every three or four weeks for several months until Rainbow Network had enough money to start a full-blown project – or network – in the San Ramon area.

But malnutrition can have long-lasting effects. While the immediate response saved lives, there were lives that continued to need medical intervention.

In 2003, Dr. Candido saw a toddler named Alejandro Josue Fajardo Gonzalez in El Carmen. But Alejandro was not toddling. Despite being about three years old, Alejandro had never walked. When he was not yet a year old, he suffered severe back pain that sent his parents to a doctor who told them the baby had had a stroke. With no money for medical treatment, all they could do was take their baby home and watch him languish.

Then Rainbow Network arrived, and all of that changed. The boy was examined, but this time the doctors said his problems were not caused by a debilitating stroke but by severe malnutrition. He was immediately treated with needed medications, thanks to Rainbow donors, and put on a nutritious diet. Four months later, he was walking.

"I felt so happy," says his father, also named Alejandro. "We are poor. We were unable to buy those treatments, those medicines. We were worried. It all changed when Rainbow Network came."

Alejandro's six siblings were also able to eat at the feeding center and attend the Rainbow school. Alejandro now attends high school on a Rainbow scholarship.

Today, Alejandro is a handsome, healthy teenager who loves to play soccer. But he says his favorite thing to do is study. He hopes to attend the university and become an engineer.

"That would be such an achievement for the family," says his father.

That is my idea," adds his mother, Genara. "My plan is to see him one day in the university."

Alejandro is confident "that will happen – because of God's help."

The San Ramon Network is now fully functioning, with several thriving communities and about 400 cement block homes in Rainbow housing projects, but many lives were saved in those early days. Many children were near death when Rainbow Network arrived.

Today the challenges are great, but the progress is even greater. Where illiteracy dominated, there are now hundreds of high school graduates and thousands of children studying in the Rainbow grammar schools. Where malnutrition, pneumonia, internal parasites and diarrhea once ravaged families, Dr. Candido can now confidently say that they are healthy communities.

* * *

Miracles Found in Tragedy

Sometimes, the miracle is not that someone's life is saved, but that even a short life can have great meaning. That is what happened in the case of Margine Carmen Diaz Davila.

Residents of Margine's community of Los Pinos, as well as Rainbow staff, all smile at the memory of that teenage girl who represented the hope that is found only in God.

Margine's family is poor. Her father, Antonio, earned only $3 a day to care for her and her five sisters, so when Rainbow Network arrived, their biggest blessing was the opportunity to go to school. Margine became an excellent student with a passion for learning. Her mother, Angela, says she had initiative, wanted to study and loved soccer.

Then, when she was 13, things took a sharp turn when the active, bright Margine began getting sick. She had stomach pain, with vomiting and fever, as well as jaundice. The Rainbow Network medical team advised testing to make sure she got the right care.

The test results were devastating. Margine had autoimmune hepatitis, a rare condition in which the body's defenses attack the liver. Despite the grim prognosis, Margine completed high school and continued to dream of attending nursing school. Unfortunately, her condition worsened, and she was unable to realize that dream.

None of that ever dampened Margine's spirit. Although she was not able to continue her education, she encouraged her classmates. "She was very cheerful," her mother recalls. "Even though she was a girl, she acted like an adult already, advising her classmates. She always said, 'I dream about all these young people getting prepared for careers.' Thank God, one of her classmates is already studying medicine in Leon. Her uncle is studying nursing. Some are studying agronomy, civil engineering.

"A lot of classmates took her advice and are doing it. They really admired her. They mourned her death. The entire community really appreciated her."

Thanks to Rainbow Network, Margine lived 11 years after her diagnosis. "Rainbow Network was like the bridge for her to live," Angela says. "She passed away at 5 a.m. on a Saturday. The Rainbow folks all came; all the staff came; everyone came. I appreciate what they did for me, and they are still doing it."

Margine's memory and the impact she had on her community continues.

"I always say, she's not dead. She still lives," says her mother. "There is a saying, her body passed away, but her soul is alive because she passed away with Christ."

Something to Think About

Read: Acts 8:9-25

1. As a youth what did you aspire to be?
2. What had Simon been in our Scripture Lesson for today?
3. He was amazed at what? (Verse 13)
4. Why would we say that he was still learning? (Verses 18-19)
5. Do you think he had a change of heart? Explain.
6. How can you be a part of the miracles that are taking place in Nicaragua through Rainbow Network?

It was the "hand of God" that led Luke Nixon to Nicaragua. A brochure in a church pew and an invitation to travel and a little boy who couldn't walk turned Luke into a Rainbow Network supporter.

CHAPTER ELEVEN

HOW YOU CAN HELP

U.S. doctors have been very generous to Rainbow Network and the people of rural Nicaragua. Dr. Will Moore, a current board member, has visited the region numerous times, bringing other medical personnel with him to help with medical clinics, as well as physical rehab technicians who provide invaluable services to the patients and staff.

Those medical mission trips have a big impact on individuals who travel to Nicaragua, including two young volunteers, Cole Ratliff and Mahala Walker. The 18-year-olds joined a medical team from Hazard, Kentucky, where Cole's dad, Dr. Darian Ratliff, practices.

Dr. Ratliff said that he figured the trips would either make Cole give up the idea of being a doctor or convince him that medicine is the career path for him.

It convinced him. "It made me want to be a doctor even more," Cole said, as Mahala nodded in agreement. "I want to help these people."

But you don't have to be a doctor to help change lives in Nicaragua. Sometimes God uses people in surprising ways.

Luke Nixon sees the "hand of God" in his involvement with Rainbow Network and Joiner. It all actually happened many years before he had ever even heard Joiner's name. He stumbled upon a Rainbow Network brochure in the book rack of the pew at church one Sunday morning, and he began to send a monthly donation.

He often got mailings from Rainbow, along with a thank you letter, but he usually tossed them without even reading them. His business was growing, and he was busy with life.

Then he got a phone call from Rainbow Network inviting him to Nicaragua. It was the last thing he expected, and it caught him off guard, so he put the caller off with an "I'll think about it." But when he called his wife, he said, "Apparently, I'm supposed to go to Nicaragua."

Four months later, he was in Nicaragua with a group of supporters on a "Go & See" visit. Each day they went to another community to see the work Rainbow was doing, but Luke still didn't understand why he was there.

It was the last day of the visit, when the group was visiting a medical clinic that he saw a woman carrying a young child whose feet were turned in and was unable to walk. A physician who was traveling with the group explained that it was club feet. "He said, 'He will never walk'," Luke recalls. "That bugged me."

When he returned home, he called the Rainbow office to inquire about the boy, Ervin, and asked what he could do to help. "So, I donated the money for surgery," he says. Ervin is now in his teens, "a wonderfully healthy boy that loves to play soccer."

Luke was convinced that Ervin was the reason he was compelled to visit Nicaragua, but he would later learn that God had much more in store for him. He continued to be a Rainbow supporter and would often visit the website to keep up with the special medical needs program. It was on one of those visits that he learned what God had in mind. "There was Joiner staring back at me."

He called and asked about the case, learning that doctors were recommending amputation. "I remember just being horrified," he says. He spoke with Keith, who assured him that some U.S. doctors would evaluate the case. They proposed some solutions that led to Joiner's surgeries, which were much more complicated than just club feet.

"I said, I'm in, let's go," Luke recalls. "It was a fairly considerable amount of money, but I considered it an honor."

Luke sent his first check for $5,000 and continued to send whatever was needed to complete Joiner's medical care. He even sent him coloring books!

Luke has yet to return to Nicaragua. He has never met Joiner or seen Ervin since his surgery, but he is sure that they are why he got that phone call and why he had to say yes. "I was being told I was supposed to go to Nicaragua," he says with certainty. "And those two little boys, they can have families and be productive members of society now."

Individual Rainbow supporters like Luke have stepped up to respond to a special medical need. One never knows what will touch a person's heart. It may be an illness that has impacted that person's life in the past, or simply the realization that for a small financial sacrifice someone's life could be saved.

Like National Avenue Christian Church, which made it possible for Iris Karina to see and Harvin to walk, many churches focus on specific communities, and they will respond to a special medical need in that community.

Rainbow Network supporters receive regular newsletters and special medical needs are often included. The website also includes a link to the special needs. That is where Luke found Joiner.

Organizations such as Vitamin Angels, which provides vitamins for children, World Concern, which provides anti-parasite medicine from a pharmaceutical company in the Netherlands, Nica Salud, a Nicaragua-based NGO that focuses on health, and USAID, a U.S. government program, and many others partner with Rainbow Network to support the medical programs.

As the Rainbow Network doctors and staff work hard to respond to all the medical needs in the more than 140 Rainbow communities, God works in the hearts of God's people to answer their prayers.

Something to Think About

Read: Matthew 28:16-20

1. Do you remember when you got your first Bible? Explain.
2. Dr. Candido says that Rainbow Network introduced him to the Scriptures. Who introduced you?
3. Keith Jaspers, founder of Rainbow Network, says the ministry was founded upon Matthew 25:31-46. Read that passage. What are the needs listed therein of the "least of these?"
4. Why do you think the righteous did not know that they had ministered to the Lord?
5. In whom does the Christ appear to us today? List them.

For many of the residents of Rainbow Network partner communities, the Rainbow clinic is the first time they have had regular access to health care.

Education

...The advantage of knowledge is that wisdom preserves the life of him who has it.

Ecclesiastes 7:12b

Alba de los Angeles Calero grew up too poor to go to school, but when Rainbow Network arrived, she was able to get a scholarship for high school and teacher's college. Now she teaches the children in her community so they can succeed, too.

CHAPTER TWELVE

CHANGING LIVES AND COMMUNITIES

Alba de los Angeles Calero grew up in the tiny community of Piedra Rajada, where the 135 residents live in homes with dirt floors and mud walls and almost no one had an education.

Today, Alba is helping to change all that.

When Rainbow Network arrived in the remote mountain community in 2007, Alba was already a young woman. She was resigned to not being able to continue her studies because of her family's extreme poverty. Despite a gap of several years since she had completed elementary school, she was thrilled with the chance to attend high school on a Rainbow scholarship. Although she also has two brothers, Alba was the only one in her very poor family to get an education. Her brothers went to work in the fields as soon as they finished elementary school to help support their elderly parents.

To get her education, Alba had to walk the seven kilometers to the Normal Mount Zion School in the El Prado community. Then, like all Rainbow scholarship students, she would tutor the younger children back in Piedra Rajada. She grew to love education and teaching, and she did so well that she earned a Rainbow Network scholarship to attend the National Institute to get her teaching degree. That meant she had to walk a mile and get on a bus to travel the 30 miles to school. Despite often inaccessible roads during the rainy season, Alba never gave up on her dream.

After graduating, she got a job teaching about 40 students in the same school she attended at El Prado, still walking or riding her bicycle the seven kilometers. And she still teaches the children of Piedra Rajada and teaches adults how to read and write. She also helps the doctors during patient consultations by searching out the appropriate records, following the example of her mother who is an active volunteer and cooks in the community nutrition center.

Alba and the other residents of Piedra Rajada are excited about the future for their community and they wanted to show their appreciation.

It was a hot, dry February day when Johnny Moneymaker and his wife, Linda, were surprised by the the the residents of the little community.

Johnny, who is a Rainbow board member and longtime supporter, learned about the need for a new school and community center in Piedre Rajada. He pledged that if the community could get the land, he and his business partner, Mike DeLacy, would provide the materials to build the center.

When Rainbow Director Nelson Palacios took an unexpected turn down a familiar dirt road off the highway, Johnny and Linda saw a group of people carrying a large handwritten sign. They worried that it was some type of protest, but as they drew closer, they saw that the sign was thanking them for their support. The group of Piedra Rajada residents had been waiting out in the sun to share their excitement about the new community center they would build on the very land adjacent to the road where they were standing. The land had been donated by an elderly woman in the village, and she was there to give Johnny a hug.

Everyone walked back up to the village where Alba was inside a small, dark adobe building filled with desks and children, all doing school work. The children grinned as the tall American stepped inside. Two girls stood up and sang a duet, thanked Johnny and told him that they are praying for him.

The usually stoic Johnny was brought to tears. His voice cracked as he said that he just wanted to thank Jesus for bringing them together.

Alba stood smiling because she knew that the work of Rainbow Network, in the name of Jesus Christ, has made such a difference for her and her community. The new center would be built to not only house her little school, but also be used as a nutrition center, medical clinic, meeting place and worship center.

A few months after Johnny's surprise, the community center was completed, and the government accepted it as a public school site. And Alba was hired as the teacher!

Alba's own life mirrors the life of her community. Before Rainbow arrived, she was destined to a life of poverty, with only a basic elementary education. "Education and food, those two things are basic," she said. "We didn't have that before."

She understood the importance of organizing to work with Rainbow Network in 2007 when she was only about 20 years old. She stepped up as a community leader. Now she is helping her family and her community by contributing as a teacher and a leader.

"Before, it was difficult to find a teacher to teach in the community," she said. "Now, thanks to God and Rainbow Network, there are two teachers, both of us from the community. That is an achievement."

With education, healthcare and economic development through micro loans available in Piedra Rajada, the community can see a much brighter future. If land can be secured, a Rainbow housing project could mean people like Alba could get their own home instead of living with eight people in one small house, and others who need better housing could move into a secure Rainbow home.

Alba is now the mother of toddler Juan Carlos, and she has dreams for her son. "My dream is that, hopefully, I will be able to save money to provide for his education," she said. "If not, I will apply for a scholarship so that he can get an education like I did."

The scholarships, schools, nutrition centers, medical clinics and micro loans that are available to Rainbow Network communities have made a difference in Alba's life and the life of Piedra Rajada. Alba loves to tell people about the many benefits that Rainbow provides.

"I tell people that with the love and care that we get from Rainbow Network, we have a better life and a safer place."

* * *

Fulfilling your destiny

There are so many stories of lives changed thanks to the opportunity to get an education. For some, it has meant earning enough to support a family. For others, it has given meaning to their lives.

For the people in the following profiles, it has meant fulfilling a destiny to be a leader who helps change entire communities.

Ervin Maugdiel Ruiz Cortedano was the first scholarship student in his community of Santa Martha, and he was the first to go on to get a university education.

Now, the 27-year-old father of one teaches other students in the community of Hilapo. He leaves his house every morning at 6 to make the two-hour trek to his school. There, he greets his 36 elementary students with a smile and sometimes even a song.

It was his work as a Rainbow tutor that showed him how much he loved teaching and led him to a career in education.

"I like working with children," he said. "I like when I know my students are learning how to write, how to read, and when they start socializing."

If Rainbow Network had not come into Santa Martha, Ervin would be working in the fields next to his father, brothers and neighbors. He recalls that when Rainbow arrived in his mountain community the economic situation was "really, really tough."

Being able to get a high school education changed all that for Ervin. He was able to get a job in the coffee plantation, but not as a field laborer. He was put in charge of payroll. That work allowed him to pay for his university education.

He shares his story with his students, telling them how he would help his mother and work in the coffee fields before going to school in the afternoon. He tells them about the joy he took in teaching the younger children at the Rainbow Network school in Santa Martha.

He looks forward to the day his 5-year-old son, Janer, will start school. He hopes to be able to send him to high school, but knows that Rainbow will be there if he needs financial help. "I want to help him out in his education so he can get a career," Ervin said. "I would teach him how to do it. It's not really hard if he really wants to do it."

Ervin's mother always believed in her sons, he said. "She is really proud of me and my other brothers. She got three teachers as children. We are all three working as teachers, and we got together and were able to build a new house for her. She only went through the third grade."

* * *

Giving Back to Your Community

Auner Medal is a lawyer. The 28-year-old lives and works in the small community of San Isidro.

"I grew up here," he says. "We come from a humble and poor family. My mother was a single mom. She made a lot of sacrifices to provide elementary school for me."

But with four children, paying for high school was beyond her means … until Rainbow Network arrived. Auner was able to attend high school on a Rainbow scholarship. His sister and two brothers were also able to finish high school. One is now an accountant and the other is studying business administration.

Auner was also able to attend a Rainbow Network group called Young Entrepreneurs that helped members learn the skills and techniques to start a business. He took everything he learned and put together a business plan. With a micro loan, he was able to build a chicken coop.

Working closely with the Rainbow Network staff and other successful business people, he learned techniques for managing the chickens. "Thanks to God, I succeeded," he says with pride. He now has four coops, raising 600 chickens. His mother now earns a living working for him.

He raises the chicken for meat. "Since I am very well known in the area for producing high quality chickens, people buy from me," he says. Most of the meat is sold to his neighbors, but some is also sold to restaurants. In fact, his brother runs a restaurant up the road and is one of his customers, as is a cousin who has a restaurant in Managua.

"I saw I was getting profits, so I thought to myself, maybe it's time to go to school," he says. In fact, he earned enough to pay for a university education and a law degree. "I always dreamed of becoming a lawyer, in order to help other people," he says. "I was able to meet this goal."

One important thing he does for his neighbors is work to untangle the legal jumble they experience when it comes to property. Many of them have no deeds or other documents to prove they own property that has been in their family for generations.

"When it comes to legalizing your land, it's very expensive and can take a long time," he explains. "So, many people don't do it because they don't have the money for it. Sometimes you see an injustice. I would step up and help out."

Always learning, Auner is now taking an English course. "I think English is so important now," he says.

One of the ways he hopes to use his English skills is writing contracts for some of the many NGOs in Nicaragua. He would also love to do legal work for Rainbow Network. "It would be such a pleasure for me," he says.

Helping Rainbow Network would be a way that Auner could give back to the organization for all the help it has brought to him and his community.

"I'm so grateful to Rainbow Network because I think that they helped me form myself, not only professionally, but also spiritually," he says.

His community has also been transformed. Twenty-one families in San Isidro have been able to get safe Rainbow houses. "I consider this such a blessing," says Auner. "And many people are being benefitted with an education."

He admits that not everyone has taken advantage of the opportunities offered, so he tries to encourage them. "Rainbow Network opened the doors to me when I needed it, and I was able to take good advantage of that," he says. "I always tell people, 'You always have to think about meeting your goals, go to a higher level.' ...

"If I was able to make it, they can make it too."

* * *

Never Giving Up

Celso Enrique Martinez lives with his family in La Grecia. He is an example of determination and leadership.

It took him seven years to get a Rainbow Network scholarship to go to high school, and now – at 32 – he has applied for a scholarship to go to university. Although financial need has often sent him back into the coffee fields to work, he has always loved school and still plans to continue his education.

Celso calls himself a "born social worker." He has studied social work and especially liked the fact that it allows you to work in and help your community. It is something he already does.

For example, when he learns that someone is sick, he visits the family and finds out what they need. "That is how you grow as a leader," he says.

Celso goes a step further. "When someone passes away in my community, I'm the one who prepares the body," he says. "I am not afraid to do that. I'm OK with that."

He serves as the community coordinator for Rainbow Network and has headed up the committee that is working on getting potable water into La Grecia. Helping his community and his family – and someday having a family of his own – is an important focus of Celso's life. "As a leader, sometimes you might find a situation is not always blossoming," he admits. "You might confront hardships. That is where you need to use your strategies, look for support or help."

But, at the heart of it all, the most important thing that is needed is education, he says. "I would say that is one of the foundations of the country. That is how you can improve your qualify of life. Even though you're not going to be able to totally eradicate poverty, you might improve the level of life."

Something to Think About

Read: Matthew 5:1-12; Mark 10:1

Jesus, the rabbi, *taught* wherever He went. He believed that education was very important!

1. How has education been crucial in your life?
2. What value do you place on it?
3. Were you ever ready to give up on getting an education? Explain.
4. What is a favorite story for you out of Nicaragua in this regard?
5. What role does persistence play?
6. How is the Rainbow Network Education Program a "hand up, not a handout?"
7. If you grew up in the extreme poverty, so prevalent in Nicaragua, what would be the challenges both mentally and physically for you to rise to a level of self-sufficiency?

The children at Divina Infantita get love, a home and an education, thanks to the sisters who run the orphanage and school. Rainbow Network has helped Divina Infantita financially and by providing school teachers.

CHAPTER THIRTEEN

CARING FOR THE ORPHANS

The impact of Rainbow Network's education programs reaches well beyond the little communities within the networks. It touches lives throughout Nicaragua.

The Divina Infantita Orphanage in El Crucero is home to about 30 children, with many more attending school there. For many of them, this is the only safe place they have. Some have been rescued off the streets; others are brought there by grieving family members who cannot take care of the children.

Mother Superior Griselda came here in 1993, then only a teenager herself, to help open the orphanage, reaching out to children who have no family or are victims of poverty and violence. But less than 10 years later, the orphanage and school almost had to close.

Keith Jaspers tells the story of Rainbow Network's arrival in El Crucero in 2001 when he learned how the former Mother Superior had fallen for an email scam and lost $10,000, putting the future of the orphanage at serious risk. The school also faced closure by the government because its teachers were not sufficiently educated and the leaders had no university degrees.

Rainbow Network replaced the stolen money and also addressed the lack of educated staff. A scholarship sent Griselda to university to study psychology, and many of the nuns were able to complete their education and leave the convent to work out in the community. Rainbow provided 12 scholarships to the nuns and students who would not have otherwise been able to attend high school. In fact, the current Mother Superior is a Rainbow scholarship student herself!

The teaching staff are all lay teachers now, and four of the school's current staff were able to get their education through Rainbow Network scholarships and are thrilled to be able to give back by helping the children at Divina Infantita.

And the sisters and children in the orphanage continue to get assistance from Rainbow Network, including food and healthcare.

* * *

Sharing Your Story

Lidieth del Socorro Arauz Hernandez learned about Rainbow Network when the organization came to her community in 2003 when she was about 13. The oldest of five children, she had to stop attending school after completing the sixth grade. Rainbow scholarships meant she could go on to complete high school and even get a university degree in education in 2011.

Like all the Rainbow scholarship students, she taught at the Rainbow school in the afternoon. There she saw her future as an educator. It was her love of children and the opportunity to help them through their own problems that convinced her to become a teacher.

She started teaching in Managua but was able to return to El Crucero to teach. She now teaches 29 students in the second grade at Divina Infantita.

She is a natural in the classroom, calling out "Buenos dias" as she enters. Her young students warmly respond. Her love for her students is manifest in many ways, including her farewell when she steps out of the classroom, "Adios amor."

She wants them all to understand how important education is, so she shares her story with her students, not just the ones who have struggles, but even those whose families are able to send them to school.

"I teach this to my students, especially those who have no trouble going on to school, so that I can show them how difficult success is for you if you don't have anything," she says. "My grandmother and grandfather took care of me, but they didn't have the money for a better life. I say to them that they need to appreciate the work their parents do for them. It was Rainbow Network who helped me."

She lives in the community of Los Fierros, where she serves on the education committee.

Now Lidieth is a mother herself, with a young son. "In the future, I want to tell him about my experience, to be responsible and work and improve his life. I want to support my son, give him all my support, because my parents did not do that for me," she says.

Her job provides a stable life and steady income for her family. Her husband is a construction worker, so his work is sporadic.

But the economic security is not what makes Lidieth love her job. Her favorite thing is watching her students succeed. "You know you are doing the right thing when they respond," she says.

* * *

Returning the Favor

Sophia Espinoza teaches the kindergarten class at Divina Infantita. She was able to attend high school through a Rainbow scholarship and, at age 29, graduated from college, also with the help of a Rainbow scholarship. She was sponsored by Acts Ministry in Missouri, and teaching at the orphanage is the perfect way for her to repay that help.

"I love to teach," she declares. She began as an assistant to a nun in the preschool and was given the opportunity to teach one group because she did so well. She is now in charge of a classroom with 26 students.

"Juanita del Carmen Perez, who worked with Rainbow Network as a coordinator for education and economic development, mentored Sophia and showed her how to improve her life," Sophia says. Because Sophia's parents abandoned her as a child, she appreciated that Juanita showed her love and acceptance and convinced her that she was a valuable person.

Now Sophia is returning the favor. She not only passes that love on to her students, she helps in her community, especially with the health program. A micro loan allowed her to open a small bookstore in San Ramon. Her 12-year-old daughter is also attending high school on a Rainbow scholarship.

Sophia continues to support Rainbow Network by teaching in the community and helping the "poor street children without family to protect them."

She knows the difference that kind of support can mean. "I am very thankful," she says. "Without the help and support of Rainbow Network, I would not have this education. God bless Rainbow Network."

* * *

A Happy Heart

Rodrigo Antonio Romero teaches sixth grade and physical education. "I love it because the children trust me," he says. "I also see more confidence in the children."

Rodrigo was able to complete high school and get a teaching certificate through Rainbow scholarships and will complete his university degree in 2017. He and his mother also received a micro loan to open a small bookstore in the community of San Ramon.

It was his mother who encouraged him and told him how important education is. And it was his love for children that made him decide that teaching was the best way to make sure others also got a good education.

He is at ease even with strangers and jokes easily.

Rodrigo's easygoing nature and humor have made him a favorite among the students and at home. "I love to share a good time with people," he says with a grin.

The opportunity to work at Divina Infantita, has been important, too. "This experience is excellent," he says. "This makes my heart feel good."

* * *

A Heart to Help

Karla Patricia Romero teaches sixth grade at Divina Infantita. She also serves on the education committee and teaches adults in San Ramon.

"I have seen a lot of change, a lot of support in education," says Karla, who has been teaching for 14 years. She is proud that San Ramon has produced three teachers at Divina Infantita. "Rainbow Network also builds houses, gives scholarships and micro loans, all to help families."

Karla has been the recipient of those services. She has had numerous micro loans for a small business she runs out of her home. She has sold school supplies and made photocopies for customers, and now she sells clothing. The extra income helps her support her family.

Karla's 4-year-old son, Fabricio Antonia Romero, stops in her office to beat on a drum with a complicated rhythm and then gives his mother a smile. She smiles in return and sends him back to his classroom.

"Rainbow Network has the love and heart to help people find the root of the problems and fix what is going wrong," Karla says. "It increases teamwork. They encourage you to work for yourself and succeed in your way."

Divina Infantita is just one example of many that demonstrates Rainbow Network's long reach into Nicaragua. Rainbow scholars have become teachers and administrators in schools around the country, making sure that other students get a good education. They have also made it possible to open schools in isolated regions where children previously had to walk many kilometers to reach an available classroom.

Something to Think About

Read again: Matthew 25:31-46

1. In Jesus' depiction of the Last Judgment, who are the "least of these?"
2. Who are the least of these in our world today?
3. What does Love demand of us in their regard?
4. What is the role of providing an education play in all of this? Explain.
5. Teachers producing more teachers: What does that mean for children in Nicaragua?
6. It you could be granted one wish for the children of Nicaragua, what would it be?
7. What would Jesus have you do?

When Maria Elsa Ruiz Vallejos was just a child, she had to work in the coffee fields to pay for her education. Now, she is a regional supervisor for Rainbow Network, overseeing three networks, and supervisor for education for the entire organization.

CHAPTER FOURTEEN

A Word of Hope

Maria Elsa Ruiz Vallejos grew up in the tiny rural community of La Grecia where her family lived in poverty. Her father died when she was just 13 years old, leaving her mother to raise eight children.

"It was a very tough life," she says. She contributed the money she went out to pick coffee to contribute to her family and to have money to attend school. "It was hard. When I was growing up, there was no Rainbow Network for a scholarship."

Maria Elsa persevered, working days and attending high school at night. "It was tough, but I wanted to get ahead," she says.

Today, she is a regional supervisor for Rainbow Network, overseeing three networks, and supervisor for education for the entire organization. She is married, with a 14-year-old daughter who is in her third year of high school.

She was an elementary school teacher when she learned about Rainbow Network in 2002. "I was actually teaching in the communities where Rainbow was coming to work," she says. "So I learned about Rainbow, how it was coming to these communities with all the help that I knew these families needed. All of that inspired me, so I applied for a job. I wanted to be part of that work, the great work that Rainbow had been doing in Nicaragua."

Her work as a teacher and her desire to help the people in the community made Maria Elsa the perfect choice as coordinator for the education program. She recognized the need and the impact education could have on the students and the community.

"Many of the scholarship students didn't have any chance to continue their studies if Rainbow Network had not come into their communities," she says. She saw her job as a way to "contribute to these people so they could meet their goals and dreams."

She was later promoted to manager of the network in San Ramon and recently took on the regional position. "I continue to support the work that we do in the communities. I work with all the components – education, housing, micro loans ... to support every one of the managers in the different networks."

The work takes her to many communities, working with the leaders and the parents, attending meetings, setting up workshops and seeing the difference all that work is making in the lives of people of rural Nicaragua.

"What touches me is to be able to help the families that need the most," she says. "These families have at least a word of hope."

She sees the changes in their lives – Harvin being able to walk and his family able to live in a secure Rainbow house; Margine's desire to help her community even as she faced death; Celso getting an education and becoming a leader in his community despite struggles and setbacks.

Maria Elsa has never stopped working with and caring about education. Every day she sees families who face hardship, living in conditions that take one's breath away. Rainbow Network addresses many of those needs through its health, housing and micro loan programs, but it is the education component that Maria Elsa sees as the cornerstone of change.

So she wants to be the source of encouragement that her mother was for her when she was working days and going to school nights. The payoff, for Maria Elsa, is simple:

"Just to see that these young people have a job, one that they got through education provided by Rainbow Network."

Something to Think About

Read: Matthew 12:15-21

See page 99 for discussion questions.

These young women are able to get an education, thanks to Rainbow Network scholarship supporters.

Education is one of the most important elements of the Rainbow Network model. Children not only learn at Rainbow schools, they can get scholarships to high school and beyond. And they get a nutritious meal every school day.

CHAPTER FIFTEEN

How It Works

When Keith and Karen Jaspers started Rainbow Network in 1995, the goal was to provide housing using the Habitat for Humanity model. But they quickly realized that it would take more than housing to help rural Nicaraguans move out of poverty. Someone was sick in nearly every household. No one had the resources to earn a decent living for their families. Few people were getting even the most basic education.

If Nicaraguans were going to be able to help themselves and their communities, they would need some tools. Education is a tool that can do many jobs, so Rainbow Network looked for a way to help provide that tool.

In Nicaragua, the government ensures that all children get a free education, but in remote rural areas, that education is often unreachable – physically and economically.

The ubiquitous one-story, blue and white block buildings announce that it is the location of a school. Unfortunately, some of them don't have teachers, and some small communities don't even rank a building. This means that children must travel many miles to get to a staffed school where there may not be enough desks or books, and there are likely to be 40-plus students to a single teacher.

With dirt roads that often become treacherous in the rainy season, few available vehicles and uncertain buses, making it to school and home again is often difficult, if not impossible, especially for very young children. The cost of transportation and school supplies, as well as worries about food and proper clothing and shoes, add to that difficulty.

And, when families are struggling to eat, every hand is often needed to do the backbreaking field work that will at least bring in enough money to buy food and basics. School takes a backseat.

While elementary school education is compulsory, the government does not enforce the law, especially among families that are likely to need their children to work, so many people get only a sporadic education.

It is even more difficult to attend high school, which may only be available in a larger town. Uniforms, books and school supplies,

95

transportation and food can make the cost of a high school education unattainable for poor families.

Higher education, whether a normal school for teachers, technical school or university, is well beyond the possibility for most families in rural Nicaragua without some outside financial assistance. At the elementary and high school level, school meets from February or March to November or December. Most elementary schools meet only in the morning, while high school schedules can vary, including evenings or weekends.

Rainbow Network recognized a way to address many of the failings of this education system. The organization could help students get a high school education and use those scholars to help the younger students in the afternoon. By including an afternoon meal, children would get the nutrition they needed to thrive and to learn.

The scholarship program has already seen more than 1,500 students get a diploma, some at a post-secondary level. There are now more than 1,000 scholarship students in the program.

The Rainbow Network requires each scholar to tutor the younger children after everyone is fed a nutritious lunch from the feeding center, which is staffed by local volunteers. The food generally includes beans and rice, enriched with a protein supplement drink. The locals contribute whatever produce they can add to the meal, cook it over a wood stove and serve it in plastic bowls that must be returned and washed to be filled again until everyone is fed.

Everyone – even the youngest of the students – first wash their hands thoroughly, happy to explain that they do it to prevent ingesting parasites that can cause illness and even death. Then, they wait patiently as the bowls of food and cups filled with a nutritious oatmeal drink are distributed. It often means that the older students must watch the younger ones eat first because there aren't enough bowls for everyone, but there are no complaints.

In addition to the students, pregnant and nursing mothers, young children and the elderly are invited to eat at the centers.

Where there is a public school building, the meals and the afternoon tutoring is done there. But in communities that do not have a school, a community building or even a private home is used for those services. For some young children, this is the only schooling they get because they are unable to travel to the public school.

The scholarship students have a variety of responsibilities in each community, but the most important one is their tutoring job. For many, it is the first time they have had such a significant role in their community, and it often creates leaders – as well as future teachers. In fact, many of the communities that did not have teaching staff available are now being taught by former scholarship students!

The cycle is organic. Where there was once little opportunity to get an education, there are now schools and teachers right in the poor rural communities that make up Rainbow Networks. Where there were once few, if any, people with a high school education, there are now graduates who have returned to teach their neighbors and their neighbor's children. Those graduates are also able to get good-paying jobs that support their families and lift up their communities.

Where illiteracy and lack of education kept poor families in poverty, there are now educated children who have gone on to teach others how to improve their lives.

All of the other Rainbow Network programs are hinged on education.

The students help keep the records for the doctors who visit the tiny villages, and they help families understand the doctor's orders.

The feeding centers at the schools keep children healthy so they can learn and grow up to be successful adults.

The housing program allows students to have a safe, dry place to study. Many families even set up a study area in their homes.

Many of the students are able to go on to be successful business people, using the micro loan program to start or expand their enterprises or work in their parents' businesses.

Nicaragua has struggled with its education system. It has the lowest funding rate in Central America, and political influences have created untenable situations. Although the government has pledged to improve the system, the poorest in the country are seldom the recipients of any improvements.

So, Rainbow Network has taken the lead, often working with the government to provide teaching staff and reopen schools. But the real energy is provided by the people in those communities, including the scholarship recipients.

Their stories demonstrate the struggles many of them have overcome just to get an education, and the ways that those graduates have gone on to improve the lives of so many others. This is how Rainbow Network works – because that is how God works in our lives.

"I always felt that the Rainbow Network was what God created me to do," Keith Jaspers said in a reflection on the organization's first 20 years. "Its demands match my skills. Its work matches my understanding of what the Scripture tells us to do with the poor. Its results indicate the truth of His words and prove that ordinary people doing ordinary things can have huge impacts if we follow those Scriptures."

Something to Think About

Read: Matthew 12:15-21

1. Isaiah was describing the coming Messiah in this quotation, he states: "... and in His name will the Gentiles hope." (verse 21) In what ways does Jesus give us hope?
2. What are some specific ways Rainbow Network brings hope to persons in Nicaragua?
3. C.T. Studd once declared: "Only one life, 'twill soon be past, only what's done for Christ will last." What lasting heritage are you leaving?
4. How can you partner with the Rainbow Network?

Helping a single student, by sponsoring a scholarship, can change the life of the student, his family and the donor. Personal relationships are forged through letters, and even visits, that demonstrate how important a small monthly contribution can be.

CHAPTER SIXTEEN

How You Can Help

Unlike the housing and micro loan programs, Rainbow Network's education program does not support itself through a repayment plan. The repayment is much bigger, but the immediate financial needs are met through donations from supporters.

Rainbow supporters provide the necessary funding – $30 a month – to send a student to high school. In exchange, the donor is given the name, profile and a photo of the student, and is encouraged to communicate by letters.

For some donors, it is a simple automatic deduction from their bank account or credit card to Rainbow Network each month. They do nothing more than appreciate the work that their money is doing.

For others, it can become personal. The letters are cherished, and birthday or Christmas cards become special events.

Mel and Ruth Miller of Springfield, Missouri, have never been to Nicaragua, but they have sponsored scholarship students and have come to love them. "One is a nurse now," Ruth says with pride.

"Why do we sponsor a student in Nicaragua? It is hard to put into words that don't sound cliché or downright self-serving," say Dan and Regina Bohannon of Sparta, Missouri.

"Our reason is to give a person – not some nameless student – Deyvin Jose Jarquin Zamora, the means to pursue his dream. His dream, by our American standards, may not seem too lofty. Deyvin wants to go to school. He starts his day at 5:30 a.m. and walks an hour, then catches a bus for a 15-minute ride to the nearest school. Deyvin is not compelled by the government or law to do this. Deyvin is driven by ambition to change not just his life but those of his family and his neighbors. Education in Nicaragua is a ticket to a better life. Why would we not want to help him?"

And some get to meet their scholarship student.

Mark and Dorothy Harsen, also of Springfield, became supporters in 2003 after taking a mission trip there with their church. One way they have supported the ministry is by sponsoring scholarship students.

The Harsens have traveled to Nicaragua with Rainbow five times. On one of those visits, they were able to meet one of those students who, with his father, expressed such appreciation that it touched them. "All you have to do is give up a few trips to McDonald's," says Mark. "It's not that much money. Then, to hear that father express his gratitude, I realized that it is much more than that."

When a group of supporters from Woods Chapel United Methodist Church near Kansas City, Missouri, visited Los Pinos, a community the church supports in a variety of ways; the scholarship students were there to greet them. Hugs and gifts exchanged made it seem like a reunion. Although these folks had never met before, they had developed a relationship that crossed borders and overcame distance.

The personal connection available through the scholarship program creates a bond between people and countries. The students not only succeed in school and later in life, they begin to see themselves as part of something much bigger than their small community. They and their sponsors see themselves as part of the family of God.

Keith hopes to see the work of Rainbow Network continue and expand in Nicaragua. And he dreams of a better Nicaragua.

"I yearn to see the children of so many families I know well graduate from high school and return to their home communities as future leaders and parents," he reflected. "Communities and towns are changing as our programs expand and touch more lives. Nicaragua is changing as old country habits are replaced. Opportunities are created where none existed. And, just maybe, a new president of Nicaragua is graduating from high school this December!"

Something to Think About

1. What can you do to help the children of Nicaragua get an education?
2. Take some moments to pray about your response.
3. What would a "stretch plan" be for you, and/or your group? Discuss the specifics.
4. When will you begin?

Economic Development

Let the thief no longer steal, but rather let him labor, doing honest work with his own hands, so that he may have something to share with anyone in need.

Ephesians 4:28

Camillo Marenco went from a field laborer to a farmer who employs his neighbors to help harvest his crops of pineapples. Through Rainbow Network micro loans and training, Camillo is a successful businessman and a leader in his community.

CHAPTER SEVENTEEN

LEARNING TO SUCCEED

Camilo Marenco stands in his pineapple field, high up on a steep mountainside overlooking the summit and slopes of El Crucero and remembers his life before he began working with Rainbow Network in 2005.

He worked hard in the fields for little money. Now he has a successful farming operation.

He has no education. Now his daughter is getting her bachelor's degree.

He and his family lived in a house made of sticks and plastic. Now he has a stone and block home, and he has improved his daughter's house as well.

He did not believe that there was anything more for him or his children.

"Now, not only do I provide for my family, but I provide jobs for two other families," he says.

When Rainbow came to the El Crucero community of Temoa, Camilo immediately recognized the possibilities. Despite a lack of formal education, he can read and write and is intelligent and quick witted. He took advantage of training programs offered by Rainbow, especially when other successful farmers would speak. He learned about what would grow in the volcanic acid and ash of the Sierras de Managua.

He says that he embraced what he learned from Rainbow Network, "and now it's a fact." He welcomes his visitors to sit in a shady spot in front of his home, with a colorful arrangement of the pineapples, dragon fruit and other produce he grows displayed on a table.

"I am grateful to God to share my testimony," he starts.

By 2009, he was serving as president of his community's Rainbow Network committee and got his first micro loan. His loans of 2,000 *cordobas* (about $70) were used to buy small parcels of land. First, he raised pigs and goats and made a profit. Then he moved to growing vegetables and fruit. He continued to get loans, but now he has a successful farm and no longer needs loans. In fact, people joke with him that he has enough to make loans.

"It's not that I don't need Rainbow Network," he says. "I wanted to be self-sufficient."

As a business leader in his community, Camilo owns nine *manzanas* (about 13 acres) that he was able to purchase through Rainbow Network loans and from his profits. He farms most of the land and rents the rest. He now exports his dragon fruit to Costa Rica and recently began selling his pineapples to the United States. He recognized the importance of growing organic crops and has the certification to export his fruit as organic.

Working with a company that provides him the organic compost and the certification, he is able to make a profit of 90,000 cordobas (about $3,200) on each of his seven harvests a year.

"I've been an example," he says. "I work hard and I've moved forward." Now, 35 other farmers in the area have organized to grow organics.

"I can see that we've moved forward," he says. "My community is poor. Because of the volcanic acid, we can't grow other fruit or tomatoes."

But Camilo does not take credit for all that success. "The glory is for God," he insists. "I don't see myself as rich. I can feed my family. I want to show others they can do it, as well. Rainbow Network taught me that."

Self-empowerment is an important part of Rainbow Network's economic development and micro loan programs. And Camilo is an example of what can be accomplished with a little help and a lot of encouragement.

For example, Camilo used to walk wherever he went. Rainbow Network provided him with a bicycle to make travel a little easier. Now, he owns a motorcycle and uses it to help others in the community when there is an emergency.

Giving back is an important part of Camilo's story. His success is the result of Rainbow's training programs, so he now leads training programs for others in the El Crucero network. His daughter's education was the result of a Rainbow scholarship. Like all high school scholarship students, she was required to volunteer her time helping the younger students at the Rainbow school in her community. "She fell in love with education," her father says with pride. In 2012, she started teaching in the public school. "She says she owes a lot to Rainbow Network," Camilo says. "This is a way to pay back."

All this success is also the result of hard work. Besides working in his own fields during the day, Camilo works as a security guard at night. He also grows his own garden for the family. "I don't have to pay 30 cordobas to get a squash," he smiles. "I just pick it."

He built an artisan oven outside the house where his daughters bake bread to sell in the community. His three grandchildren also know how to bake bread after they return from school.

But education comes first. "I tell them, 'I didn't get an education, so you must do it'," he says.

The future is bright for Camilo and his pineapple farm. He continues to plan for expansions and even has a savings account to support his business. And he continues to look for ways to help move his community forward.

"I have been able to empower myself and help others and the community," he says. "Rainbow Network always says to do this."

* * *

Dinner at Hairy's

Eveling and Mauricio Castro get up at about 4 o'clock every morning in order to have breakfast ready to sell by 6 a.m. out of their popular restaurant along the main road into La Lima. Then, they stay open until 10 p.m. – midnight on Saturdays – serving Eveling's famous fried enchiladas and keeping their eight pool tables busy.

You might think that the couple would complain about the long hours and hard work, but Eveling and Mauricio are happy. They own their own thriving business and have a home where they and their two daughters live.

Eight years ago, they were living with her mother, Mauricio was a field worker, and Eveling made enchiladas to sell to her neighbors to help support the family. Sending their daughters to high school or college was only a dream.

Then Rainbow Network came into their community. Eveling became the community coordinator, working hard to implement the various programs. Their daughters, Erladis and Jessica were given scholarships for high school. Two years later, they applied for a micro loan.

First, they bought some pigs to raise and slaughter, selling the meat. With the profits, they were eventually able to start their restaurant, earning enough to buy a freezer and other items for the business. They put tables and chairs inside for diners and set up a small patio area in front where Eveling grills chicken, pork and beef, serving tamales, rice, beans, soups and stews, as well as her famous enchiladas.

Business flourished, with customers keeping Eveling busy dishing out heaping portions into to-go containers to people coming home from working in the fields and selling ice cream to students after school. Now, Eveling and Mauricio go to Managua to buy 220 pounds of chicken for their business.

Next to the restaurant area is a small pulperia where customers can walk up to the window to buy snacks and cold drinks.

And on the other side is the pool room, an airy covered deck with a spectacular view and eight pool tables – bought with micro loans and lovingly restored by Mauricio. Soon they hope to expand, building the deck out over the steep hillside, to add more tables.

Eveling says the name of the business is Eveling's. "But some people call it El Peludo, The Hairy One," Mauricio adds with a grin and pointing to his long hair braided down his back, full beard and hairy arms.

While their first loan was only $180, they now get some of the largest loans. Most recently, they each got loans for $700. Only people with really good credit and a track record of repayment can get such a large loan.

Eveling and Mauricio not only have great credit, they have a truly successful business and they are both thrilled with their new life. Mauricio no longer has to do the back-breaking field work in the coffee fields. Instead, he raises some coffee and vegetables in a garden across from the restaurant, helps Eveling and keeps the pool tables in good repair.

His constant smile is evidence of how happy he is that his family is now self-sufficient and an important part of the community. Inside the restaurant the walls are covered with their daughters' photos and copies of their diplomas. They have gone on in school and also help out at the family business.

By having access to financial assistance, this family has flourished, and La Lima has a wonderful place to gather for food and fun.

* * *

Rancher, Businessman, Father, Leader

Manuel de Jesus Martinez Alegria has a corral where his 11 cows and calves, and one bull, are kept. Each is branded with a capital M in a circle. That brand is testimony to his success as a rancher, farmer, businessman, father and community leader.

When Rainbow Network came to Las Jaguas in the Ciudad Sandino network 16 years ago, Manuel heard that it was an organization that was helping rural communities in Nicaragua. He heard that they were helping the children get an education, nourishing food and healthcare.

"I was excited when they came," he says. "We knew that was a moment for us to provide nutrition for our children."

Although Manuel had been able to go to school to study accounting and became a teacher, he was unable to earn enough to support his wife and four children. But his natural leadership skills and positive outlook were a natural fit for the Rainbow Network programs.

Soon, he was president of the community committee, and when the micro loan program was offered, he immediately applied. His first loan was only $80, to purchase a pig. "When the pig got real big, I sold it and purchased a small cow," he says. The next loan was for $200 to set up a food cart business, which he took to the baseball field during games.

With the profit from that loan, he bought an ox, but it wouldn't work, so he tried to sell it. He couldn't get enough money for it, so he slaughtered it. They ate some, gave some away and sold the rest. "I still got enough money to buy another ox and a cow," he says, adding that he learned a better business model with that experience. Since then, he has added to his herd and is going to technical school in Managua to learn more about raising cattle.

Two loans allowed him to buy a bright green truck, which allows him to drive into the city, sell firewood, get to the baseball field to work out of the food cart and provide rides for his neighbors.

He credits the micro loan program with making the biggest impact on the people of Las Jaguas. "Maybe they haven't been as successful as I have been, but I see them working hard and trying to succeed," he says. He points out that Las Jaguas now has electricity but still lacks a sufficient water supply. He is working toward that goal ... and more.

"But the vision that I have is a baseball field for recreation," he says. "We could also build a playground for the children."

In addition to chairing the Rainbow committee, he is president of an agricultural cooperative that grows rice, beans and sorghum. The land is owned by 15 family partners, each farming on five *manzanas* (about 8.7 acres). To get to the land, Manuel climbs up the mountainside along unstable terrain, but he makes the trip regularly to tend the crop.

His whole family works hard, including his wife, Carmen Maria, who gets up at 4 a.m. to make enchiladas and fried pork pieces called *chanfaina* to sell at the baseball game two Sundays a month, bringing in about $25 for her work.

"We need to find a way to survive one way or the other," she says.

The hard work doesn't bother Manuel. He smiles and laughs freely and, on the way back from his field, even takes time to show off how he can balance a large gourd on his head while he does a little jig.

Manuel is a natural businessman who always knew he could succeed. "But Rainbow Network is how we've been able to succeed," he says. "I really thank God and Rainbow Network. It's only because of them that I have been able to succeed."

Something to Think About

Read: Matthew 11:1-15

1. For those of you who are married, when did you decide that this is "the one" for you?
2. When you shop for a church, what tells you that this is "the one" for you?
3. Who questions if Jesus is the Messiah he or she has been looking for? Why did John question do you think?
4. What criteria does Jesus give to determine that He is the Messiah?
5. How was John different than the well-groomed preacher of our day?
6. What does Jesus say about John?
7. Who did Jesus say would have the good news preached to them?

Weaving hammocks is a traditional skill in some communities in rural Nicaragua. Rainbow Network has helped families learn how to maximize their hammock-making business and help their neighbors learn to do the same.

CHAPTER EIGHTEEN

CHANGING LIVES

There are many more stories of changed lives because of Rainbow Network's micro loan program. As in the stories above, the loan program, guidance and training offered through Rainbow Network has impacted individuals, extended families and even communities.

That is the case in the community of San Pedro where a Rainbow housing project not only provided safe, secure homes for families, it provided space for commerce. The residents of San Pedro share a unique talent: They make hammocks.

When Rainbow Network arrived, staff found five families who made hammocks and sold them in their community. Those families helped to teach others the skills, and Rainbow made the looms and set up a marketing plan. Today about 150 families in the community and neighboring Valle de San Juan make a good living making and selling hammocks.

The family of Buena Aventura Martinez and Alba Rosa Perez and their five children now have a thriving hammock business through Rainbow Network loans. The front of their home provides the space for the whole family to manufacture the colorful hammocks, which their dad sells all over Central America.

Hammocks are an important item of "furniture" in Nicaragua and other countries of Central America. They provide sleeping space that can be easily moved out of the way to allow the space to be used during the day.

The Martinez-Perez children are all talented hammock weavers. Ariel, 17, Estelle, 15, Cindy, 11, and Adonis, 8, all know how to run the "needle" to weave the multicolored hammocks. Little Buena Aventura is only 2 so he will need to grow a little more before he can help.

The two older children say they do not plan to be hammock makers forever. Both want to study English and use that skill to get good-paying jobs. The children all go to school, thanks to Rainbow scholarships.

When the Rainbow housing project was announced, the family quickly applied. The home where they had been living was no more than sticks and mud. "I would have to get up in the middle of the night to cover my children because we were getting wet," Alba remembers. First, Rainbow gave her sheets of plastic to help keep the rain out, then they were able to move into a new Rainbow house.

"This house is much bigger," Alba says. "I don't get wet when it rains. We are OK."

Estelle agrees. "It's nicer, and I have a nice view."

But the Rainbow Network micro loan program has expanded that impact. Dad Buena, who learned the art of making hammocks from his father and grandfather, got loans to buy materials to make the hammocks. He gets used sweaters and other knitted items, which he then unravels, cleans and straightens to create the hammocks.

He averages a profit of about $218 a month after paying for the materials, travel and accommodations in cheap hotels while he is on the road. "In a good month, you can make more," he says.

With the loan and the space in their home, the family has been able to step up hammock production. Dad then goes to larger cities, such as Leon, Managua and especially the tourist city of Granada, to sell his hammocks. He sells to stores in the marketplace, individuals on the street and takes special orders.

He also has a special license to sell his family's hammocks in Costa Rica and Honduras, where he can ask twice as much for them.

He dreams that soon his hammocks may be available in the United States! His brother-in-law is planning to travel to the U.S. to set up arrangements to sell them here. "I would like to do that," Buena admits with a twinkle in his eye.

With the help of Rainbow Network, this family went from poverty and despair to a life of hope.

* * *

Looking to the Future

Just down the road from the Perez-Martinez family, Aristides Rivas and his family live in a tidy home, with a successful pulperia in the front. His children are receiving an education, and the family now looks to the future.

Not long ago, they were living in a home of sticks and mud, built on a relative's land. "So, when Rainbow Network came in, I was one of the beneficiaries of the housing project," Aristides says with pride. "Now we are here. We have two kids and debt, but we are here."

Daughter Lizbeth Christina Rivas, 15, is in her fourth year of high school, thanks to a Rainbow scholarship, and she plans to go to university. "I just started a scholarship to study English," she says with pride. She wants to get a degree in English and become an English teacher.

Young Aristides Josua, 7, goes to elementary school and studies at the local Rainbow school. He says that he likes school but, like a typical boy, he makes a face that shows he is not really sure.

The kids help out at the pulperia while dad also works as a security guard in Sebaco, a job he calls "dangerous." Mom, Marcelles Hernandez, also buys used sweaters to provide the material to sell to her neighbors who make hammocks.

This little family are leaders in the San Pedro community. Aristides is in charge of the micro loans, and Marcelles is the secretary for the committee. Lizbeth teaches the younger students at the Rainbow school.

They all work hard to make their own life and the community stronger, taking the lead on whatever challenge lies ahead.

Aristides says he has plans to improve his family's home. "I want to make other rooms," he says. He has already built an extra bedroom in the back of the house, but it is made of tin. Soon he will rebuild it of concrete block, like the rest of the house.

Lizbeth sees education as a path to "get ahead" and become a leader.

But Aristides says that all those plans depend on God. "First of all, I ask God to provide me with life," he says.

Working with Rainbow Network has given this family an opportunity to succeed, but they are keenly aware that God is the source of life.

* * *

Spiritual Revival

The impact of having access to loans to expand economic possibilities went much further than business expansion for the people in Los Fierros. It has led to a spiritual revival!

Rainbow Network began partnering with the community in October of 2001. Soon, members of Los Fierros were benefitting from Rainbow medical clinics, feeding centers, schools, scholarships and micro loans. But the community members had been praying for a place to worship. Los Fierros flourished under the Rainbow Network program. After nearly a decade in the program, Los Fierros had developed into a good-size village, with a busy main street, businesses and homes, but there was still no church building. People were holding church services in private homes.

While Rainbow Network does build houses, the organization does not build churches. So, in 2010, Benjamin Isaias Gaitan Flores, community coordinator, president of the housing project, and pastor of one of the congregations, made a proposal. They could build their own church.

About 30 families had received micro loans from Rainbow Network and had thriving businesses. With part of the profits from their micro-loan businesses, they could buy the needed materials, and each of them could contribute their own efforts and talents to erect the building. "We had the willingness," Benjamin says. "But it was difficult."

During the week they tended to their businesses – selling *nacatamales*, enchiladas, bread and other goods – and would set aside some of those profits for the project, raising more than $10,000. Then, on the weekends, they worked on the building.

"It's worth it," Benjamin says. "Many of the brothers and sisters are feeling good about building it ourselves."

It took three long years and a lot of effort, but in 2013 Iglesia Fundamental de Jesu Cristo opened its doors. They held a dedication and thank you service to God, inviting the community – 200 came. And now there is a new Baptist church up the street!

Iglesia Fundamental de Jesu Cristo is an impressive concrete building, painted in turquoise and white, with beautifully hand-carved wooden doors leading in under a portico that displays the church's name and it's faith statement: Ephesians 2:20 – "built upon the foundation of the apostles and prophets, with Christ Jesus himself as the chief cornerstone."

Inside is a large, airy room with decorative tiles on the floor. The ceiling is exposed beams with a corrugated aluminum roof. There are plastic chairs and a simple wooden pulpit behind a table covered with a hand decorated white cloth. This is where people bring their gifts. On the stage are a drum set and speakers for the praise band.

The church has services every day except Monday and Friday. Benjamin preaches, but so do other leaders in the congregation. Each service starts with a devotional and worship songs, prayer, a welcome to visitors, personal testimonies, an offering, the lesson and more singing.

Benjamin demonstrates the acoustics by singing in a clear, confident voice, "Something is Falling Down Here."

Benjamin did not grow up as a Christian, but he had a Christian friend who invited him to church when he was a teenager. That is when he "tuned in to Jesus." He attended a Bible institute for four years to become a pastor and a church leader. In that time, his family started going with him and they are now members of Iglesia Fundamental de Jesu Cristo.

The church congregation has also grown. When the project started, there were about 30 members. That number has swelled to 70, with more than 30 children.

Through his spiritual and community leadership, Benjamin has also been able to gain the confidence of the entire community. Some even ask him to pray for them or hear their testimonies.

Benjamin thanks God for the success of his church and Los Fierros. God has worked through Rainbow Network and the many donors who support the ministry, he says.

With the Rainbow Network programs helping the families of Los Fierros to educate their children, get needed medical care and nutrition, live in safe housing and succeed in business, the spiritual growth in the community has flourished as well.

"We all work together as a team," Benjamin says. "Rainbow Network will always be welcome. ... We believe they've done good work."

Something to Think About

Read: Matthew 25:14-27

1. What financial loan, or assistance, made a big difference in your life? Explain.
2. In the Parable of the Talents, what do you credit the positive results for the persons who received five and two talents?
3. What was the problem with the one who received the one talent?
4. What are some of the businesses that persons in Nicaragua have developed because of the Loan Program?
5. How many persons have been helped, not counting families, by this program?
6. Can these receive other life-giving loans in the future?
7. What is involved for this to happen?
8. If the Master returned today, what would He say about how you have used the resources entrusted to you?

Eveling Castro creates delicious smells as she cooks up her stews and famous enchiladas outside the restaurant she and husband Mauricio started with the help of Rainbow Network micro loans. The restaurant, along with its pool tables, has given them financial success that has allowed them to get a home and send their daughters to school.

Yader Moran left his job with the government to work for Rainbow Network because he saw the difference the organization could make. Yader recalls his own poverty and hunger growing up, and it inspires him to help others.

CHAPTER NINETEEN

A Perfect Match

Yader Moran is Rainbow Network's supervisor for the micro loans and housing, but he has worked in a variety of positions since he joined Rainbow in 2003.

At that time, he was working for the Ministry of Education in Leon. In that position, he was working in La Paz Centro when a teacher in that community told him about Rainbow Network. He asked around, hoping to learn more about the organization. "They said, 'These people work with poor people.' That really got my attention," he remembers. Having studied community development and worked in that field for years, he saw this as a perfect match. He also related to those families that Rainbow serves.

"I come from an extremely poor family in a rural community," Yader says. "I grew up picking cotton in the fields, working to 6 p.m., then I went to school at night." He still lives in the rural community of El Terrero.

When Yader was 8 years old, there was no school in his community, so his father sent him to a tutor to learn to read and write. At 10, he would walk or ride a horse 12 kilometers to Los Fuentes where he tested so high, they put him in the third grade. The civil war interrupted his schooling until a Cuban teacher arrived in his community and offered classes in the evenings.

High school was 27 kilometers away, but a "godmother" took him into her home. Still, it was always a struggle. "My parents gave me notebooks, but no backpack or uniform. The only shoes I had I used for everything," he remembers. "There was no money for food. I ate breakfast, but while everyone else was eating lunch, I didn't have anything. As a teenager, you are always hungry."

After three years in the military – "Thanks to God, I didn't experience the war." – he was able to attend a technical college that the Catholic Church offered for free. He finally got regular meals! Later, he attended Normal School and got a teaching certificate.

He eventually got a job as a teacher, working for the Ministry of Education and went on to move up into administration. When he learned about the Rainbow Network opening, it meant he would have to take a cut in pay, but Yader decided it was more important to "do what you love to do."

"It has been the best opportunity," he says now. "Here, I could do what I really wanted to do."

After more than 13 years, he has seen how the work Rainbow does changes lives. "But it is more than that," he says. "There are hundreds of people who would be dead already. They now have health, thanks to Rainbow Network. We have saved lives with the health program."

Now the father of four and the proud grandfather of a grandson, Yader wishes that Rainbow Network had been there when he was going to school. But he takes joy in the fact that more than 1,800 students have finished high school in the time he has worked with the organization. "There were communities that never had a high school student before," he says. "Those are fruits from Rainbow Network."

When Yader began working with Rainbow Network, there were only 120 Rainbow houses built. By the end of 2016, that number topped 1,000. "I've been able to see where all those people lived before," says Yader. "They were living in very bad conditions. Now they live in paradise. ... Those are people who would not have been able to build a house on their own."

Education, medical care and housing are significant resources for the poor of rural Nicaragua, but Yader points out that there are many people who want to work and earn enough to support their families and communities. "But they don't have the resources. That is why Rainbow started providing micro loans. You can see that they start changing their lives."

As the supervisor for the micro loans and housing payments for all the Rainbow networks, Yader handles a lot of money and paperwork. He works closely with CEPAD – the Council of Protestant Churches in Nicaragua – to coordinate the loan program in order to meet all government requirements.

He has also worked closely with staff and loan recipients to improve the system and the past-due rate. The goal is to get the rate down to zero, he says, but points out that sometimes arrangements need to be made to work with poor families to keep them from falling behind. "The goal is that everyone becomes current," says Yader. "Keith wants that, so we have to do that. With the money we get from the interest, we also purchase medicine, so we are making people aware of this issue."

Yader has a special rapport with the residents of all the networks he visits. His ready smile and willingness to listen to their troubles and triumphs make him a welcome sight. He knows how difficult their lives can be, and he understands their faith.

"They will tell you, God is working through Rainbow Network."

Something to Think About

Read: Mark 10:17-31

1. What did Jesus say was required of this man for him to inherit eternal life?
2. In light of this lesson, what is the one thing most churchgoers lack?
3. Why do you think Jesus demanded such a response from the man?
4. Who are the rich of our world? Explain.
5. What was the rich man's response? Why?
6. In light of what Jesus said, what is required of us to inherit eternal life?
7. How does Rainbow Network help the poor of Nicaragua?

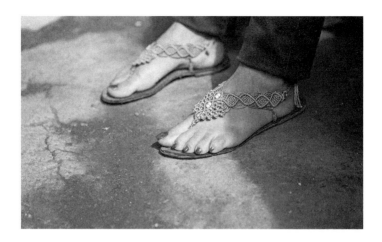

These stylish sandals are part of the inventory of a successful online business one young woman started using Rainbow Network's micro loan program.

CHAPTER TWENTY

How It Works

Micro loans are another important economic engine in Rainbow Network communities. The small cash loans provide opportunities for residents to improve their lives and for the community to take control of its destiny.

For many of these poor rural Nicaraguans, access to loans or even a bank is minimal or nonexistent, so it was important that Rainbow Network facilitate a way for people to be able to get the resources they would need to succeed.

The loans are small, now averaging about $250, but the impact is huge. For people like Camilo, the impact reaches well beyond one person or family. It changes an entire community.

But it starts with a commitment – on the part of the community and Rainbow Network. When Rainbow comes into a community, people learn that they will be responsible for their own success. Leaders are selected, and committees take on the work of organizing and managing the various programs, including the micro loan program. While Rainbow agrees to provide the money for the loans, the loan bank committee screens the loan applications and determines who will get a loan. At the same time, the committee and the other loan recipients take responsibility for repaying any bad debts in the program. That is a major commitment that is not taken lightly.

The loan program in Valle San Juan starts with a prayer to bless and guide the process as the recipients await their money. One of the bank members leads the prayer, then calls on the members of the board to promise to stand behind the loans. The contract is read and signed, with specific information about dates and payments clearly laid out.

Then the five recipients come forward and stand in front of the board, Rainbow Network representatives, family and friends, each raising his or her right hand. "We serve God," they say in unison. "We stand before you and pledge that we are going to follow the rules and will make the payments on time. We are all witnesses to this."

One little girl, about 4 years old, stands with her mother, raising her little hand, too. She already understands how important this is.

When Rainbow began making micro loans, the repayment rate was less than perfect. Now it is almost 100 percent. It wasn't that the loan process is more stringent or that more aggressive collection policies were adopted. It was the simple act of making this public promise.

"When everyone had to stand up and say, 'I promise before you and God,' our late and missed payment issues all but disappeared," Keith Jaspers says.

The micro loan program in Valle San Juan has been so successful, that it has been divided into two loan banks. This group is on its second round of loans. Each recipient has paid off his or her first loan on time and managed to make enough profit to qualify for a second loan.

A man named Castro stands to give his testimony. He explains that he was 120,000 cordobas (about $4,200) in debt, with no way to pay it back. "Rainbow Network gave me the opportunity to start working with 70,000 cordobas," he says. "And God gave me the opportunity to make the payment of 120,000 cordobas I owed and each of the loans Rainbow Network gave me."

Castro used half the money to pay on his debt and the other half for his business, a pulperia in his home. "I was able to pay it off, and my pulperia is doing great," he says with pride. With his profits, he was able to put more money into his business and buy a motorcycle. "I feel so blessed with my prosperity," he says. "I thank God and Rainbow Network."

Each loan recipient is called up by name to sign the contract and take a copy of the loan repayment plan and an envelope filled with cordobas. The first young man gets about $150 for his hammock-making business. With his young daughter in his arms, he promises to "get ahead with this loan and pay it back."

Another woman gets about $550 for her hammock business. She jokes, "That's a lot of hammocks."

The next loan is for $180, then $200, then $370. Each recipient thanks God and promises to make the payments on time. "God bless everyone," one man says. "I thank the Lord for Rainbow Network being here and providing us with the resources so we can work and move forward in this community. We really appreciate it."

The loan bank at Chichiualtepe in the El Crucero network has had at least 15 six-month loan cycles, but this year many of the recipients are new borrowers. Like those before them, they stand up together and pledge to pay on time and be responsible for all the loans, even if someone fails to pay. Then each makes his or her own pledge and tells those gathered how their loan money will be used.

One young woman makes crocheted sandals and sells them online and in the community. Another borrower is wearing a pair.

Another woman has a small pulperia, another makes "ice cream" with frozen fruit juice, and a man buys used clothes and sells them in the community. A woman makes and sells jewelry. One man grows tomatoes and sells them at a stand, using the profits to help pay for his son's education at the police academy.

An elderly man, who grows fruit and vegetables, gets $120 for supplies. He farms about 1.5 acres and, if the crop is good, he can make $2,500 in profit.

Every borrower must follow the Rainbow Network rules, but some communities have their own rules, as well. In Chichiualtepe, a borrower must pay $20 if they are late with a payment, and the group pays one person's bus fare to take the collections to the bank in the city.

While Rainbow Network provides the money to make the initial loans, the continued success of the program is dependent on loan repayment. There is no collateral required for the loans, but everyone involved understands the importance of honoring their pledge to make timely payments.

Even more importantly, each person involved recognizes that God is the true source of their success. At the beginning of the Chichiualtepe loan ceremony, a woman from the community steps up to open the meeting with prayer.

First, she thanks God for all they have been given, especially for Rainbow Network, and then asks that each of the people receiving a loan will have success. This simple faith is at the heart of everything.

Something to Think About

Read: Luke 19:1-10

1. Did you ever climb a tree as a youth?
2. What did you get out of the experience?
3. Why did Zacchaeus climb the tree?
4. What do you think were Zacchaeus' feelings when the Lord announced He was going home with him? Why?
5. When did you first meet Jesus? How did it happen?
6. How was Zacchaeus' response different from the rich man of last week's Lesson?
7. What has been your response to meeting Jesus?
8. Where does the Rainbow Network mission to the poor play out in your response to the Lord?

CHAPTER
TWENTY-ONE

HOW YOU CAN HELP

Sometimes the biggest challenge to helping is stepping aside and letting someone help themselves. That is the principle behind Rainbow Network's economic development program. Using micro loans, training programs and mentoring, the program allows Rainbow participants to become empowered to change their own lives.

Rainbow supporters have visited the various networks where individuals such as those described above have succeeded. They have seen communal efforts, such as the farming cooperative that Manuel is part of creating. There have been small factories, such as the hammock-making work in San Pedro.

Allowing the Rainbow participants to find their own path and follow it in a pure Nicaraguan way is key to creating a sustainable future for all the communities.

Embracing that concept, Rainbow supporters have been generous in their donations to the economic development programs. Through their support, micro loans have been available for most of Rainbow Network's more than 20 years working in rural Nicaragua. The loan program supports itself once it is under way, but as more communities are incorporated into the Rainbow Network family and more families are taking advantage of the program, more financial support is necessary.

That is where you come in. By making a regular monthly donation, either as an individual or a church, Rainbow Network staff in Nicaragua can find the best way to support the economic development programs, whether that is to open more loan banks, send someone to specialized training or to bring in mentors.

It is an exciting opportunity to "invest" in a fledgling business and then watch it grow and succeed. The "interest" you earn on that investment is the knowledge that your monthly or one-time donation is not only helping one entrepreneur, it is changing an entire community – and ultimately a country.

Mohammad Yunus, who was awarded a Nobel Prize in 2006 for introducing micro-lending in Bangladesh in 1976, recognized that the world's poor have all the personal resources needed to succeed. What they do not have is the economic resources.

Yunus' Grameen Bank pioneered the micro-loan program, providing small loans to impoverished people in Bangladesh so they could start and run their own businesses. Similar micro-credit projects have helped millions around the world lift themselves out of poverty.

In his book, "Banker to the Poor: Micro-Lending and the Battle Against World Poverty," he speaks of the difference between charity and empowerment. "When we want to help the poor, we usually offer them charity. Most often we use charity to avoid recognizing the problem and finding the solution for it. Charity becomes a way to shrug off our responsibility. But charity is no solution to poverty. Charity only perpetuates poverty by taking the initiative away from the poor. Charity allows us to go ahead with our own lives without worrying about the lives of the poor. Charity appeases our consciences."

Millard Fuller, founder of Habitat for Humanity and Keith Jaspers' inspiration, used that same concept to create a way that the poor could have decent housing. He also understood that to do that work, supporters would need to be willing to invest in it. His vision connected those Habitat communities and the communities of supporters around the country and the world. "For a community to be whole and healthy, it must be based on people's love and concern for each other," he said.

Rainbow Network has seen its communities thrive – become whole and healthy – thanks to the love and concern of supporters who recognize the value in helping the poor of rural Nicaragua help themselves.

It's easy to make that happen. Just go online or contact the Rainbow Network office and make a donation. The dividends are amazing!

Something to Think About

Read: Mark 12:41-44

1. As a child, did you ever watch what persons put in the offering plate?
2. What did you learn?
3. Why do you think Jesus was watching what persons put in the Temple treasury?
4. Do you think He watches what we give?
5. Why is giving important?
6. What does the poor widow teach us?
7. How might the Rainbow Network micro loan program have helped this woman?
8. What have you learned about the micro loan program that inspires you?

The Future of Rainbow Network

"For I know the plans I have for you," declares the Lord,
"plans to prosper you and not to harm you,
plans to give you hope and a future."

Jeremiah 29:11

Where We Work (2017)

CHAPTER
TWENTY-TWO

DOUBLING GOD'S BLESSINGS

Every day, struggling communities across rural Nicaragua reach out to Rainbow Network in hopes of becoming a Rainbow community, to get the help needed to reach achievable dreams for the future.

"It's always been that way, since Day One," Keith Jaspers says. "The neighboring communities want us in."

But determining the best way to use the resources available, to be good stewards of God's blessings, has always been a priority for Keith and Karen and the Rainbow Network staff and board of directors.

After 20 years of slow and steady growth and success, Rainbow Network is ready to take great strides, adding new networks, serving more communities and saving more lives.

If things go as planned and God approves, by 2024, Rainbow Network will double in size, to 13 or 14 networks.

Reaching that goal will require plenty of prayer and support. But making sure that the growth is sustainable and that the success is achievable means that careful planning and good business practices must also be followed.

Keith's own business acumen and experience and the many years of carefully managing Rainbow Network's many projects and communities have given him the insights to do that. As Keith says, he believes he was created by God to start Rainbow Network. The work not only matches his business skills, but it matches his understanding of Scripture and God's commandments to help the poor.

Keith has used those skills and understanding to create and develop Rainbow Network into a sustainable and expandable organization that can go on well beyond his personal involvement.

Rainbow Network micro loan recipients make a public oath before their neighbors and God to repay their loans and even agree to take on the debt of their fellow borrowers if they fall behind. The loan program has been an important economic engine for both the communities and for Rainbow Network.

CHAPTER
TWENTY-THREE

HOW IT WORKS

"A lot of Rainbow Network is designed to be financially self-sustainable," Keith explains. Loans are paid with interest so even more loans can be made. Houses are paid back so others can be built. Every patient that sees the doctor is charged a fee on a sliding scale from 50 cents to a dollar, if they can pay.

"All of those things generate funds," Keith says. "Collectively, those things will generate enough money to start and operate another project."

That is the plan for 2018, one more network. The cost of one new network can vary, but it is generally about a $55,000 start-up cost for vehicles, computers, office equipment and other needs. Then it will cost about $10,000 a month to operate for three to four years.

"We would not start a new network without a commitment" – either from Rainbow itself or from a donor – "that the money will be there to keep it going at least three years, but really five. It takes that long to start making significant changes," he explains.

Donors can range from a large church that can budget the monthly expense to a foundation that is willing to make that commitment. Rainbow Network is fortunate to also have some individual donors who have been moved by God and are able to donate enough to fund a network or a community.

A donor willing to finance a new network is also invited to become part of the project. For example, interested members of supporting churches often visit the network, interact with the residents even participate in some of the community meetings.

The 2018 network, which has not yet been determined, will be funded by a combination of donors and internal funding. A network location will be selected based on Rainbow Network's basic principles – a willingness on the part of the people to fully participate, the level of need and a likelihood of success. Community meetings and plenty of brainstorming at the Rainbow Network headquarters in Nicaragua and

Springfield, Missouri, will determine where a new network will be started at the beginning of 2018 and what will be done in the future. "Then we will probably stop for a year and catch our breath," Keith says. "Then start again."

In the next three years, at least three new networks, each serving 16-18 rural communities with 6,000 to 7,000 people, will become part of Rainbow Network. Then that will double over the following three years. Imagine the impact. About 40,000 poor, rural Nicaraguans will have the same opportunities to succeed that currently more than 42,000 Rainbow Network participants get. They will get a chance to purchase a safe, secure home, to read and write and see their children graduate from high school and beyond. The adequate medical care, nutrition and micro loans they receive will help them build an economic infrastructure that is currently out of reach.

The goal is 40,000 people, 500 scholarships, at least 5,000 students in Rainbow schools where nutrition centers will feed healthy lunches to children who are malnourished, 2,000 loans, 25 houses built each year as well as making available doctors will see an average of 200 people each week.

"The first battle is to get the malnutrition and parasites under control," Keith explains. Then the simple infections are treated with antibiotics or by simply changing poor sanitation habits.

"These networks will be in areas where there is very little medical help or modern medicines available. They will have poor grade schools, if any. Probably nobody is going to high school, and there are no economic opportunities for a job or a loan," he says. "Practically everybody lives in some version of a mud, stick home or hut."

Starting new networks also means hiring more staff. Rainbow supervisors, such as Maria Elsa Ruiz Vallejos, supervise three networks, but each network also needs a manager, education coordinator, loan promotor, physician and someone to do the accounting. Samuel Reyes' accounting department at the main office will also have to expand as more networks are added.

"We will have to be aggressive with fundraising," Keith admits. But much of the money – at least one third – for expansion is being raised internally. The other two thirds will come from existing and new donors.

Most of the current donors are based in the United States, but more and more are being found in Nicaragua as that country becomes more economically stable.

Under the Rainbow Network model, helping Nicaraguans succeed means empowering them with the means to help themselves and each other.

Jay Guffey, president of the Rainbow Network Board of Directors, has been a supporter since the organization's inception. Now, he hopes to help guide Rainbow Network through its next stage.

CHAPTER TWENTY-FOUR

ON BOARD WITH RAINBOW

Just as the Rainbow Network staff are all Nicaraguans (even Cuba-born Dr. Candido is now a Nicaraguan citizen!), the board will also have more Nicaraguans over the coming years. There are now two Nicaraguan board members, but that should increase to four or five, with a Nicaraguan chairman eventually.

"The decision making and heavy lifting is all being shifted to Nicaragua in the next 10 years or so," Keith explains.

Jay Guffey has been a Rainbow Network supporter since its inception. He has been on its board of directors for nearly a decade and has served as president for the past four years. He hopes to be able to be part of the organization through its next stage.

Jay's experience with Rainbow Network started at the same place Keith Jaspers started – Habitat for Humanity. He has been friends with Keith since the 1980s when Keith was on the Habitat for Humanity International board of directors.

Jay and wife Lisa were impressed with the work that Habitat was doing and began supporting the program. He joined Keith and Habitat for Humanity founder Millard Fuller on that fateful trip to Haiti in 1994. And later, Jay helped to establish an organization to help raise funds for Habitat for Humanity in a four-state region around Springfield, Missouri. He later helped to start a Habitat office in Springfield.

At that same time, he was impressed with Keith's business acumen and his desire to use those skills to do even more for people. "He saw what the opportunities were," Jay says of Keith. "He saw that Habitat didn't have all the parts. It just did housing, but it didn't help develop an infrastructure. He saw that as kind of a gap back in the 1980s."

So, when Keith and Karen started Rainbow Network in Nicaragua, Jay was excited to be a part of that. It was a way Jay and Lisa and daughters Elyse and Elayne could apply their Christian faith. Although Jay and Lisa had grown up in Christian families, it was not until they were married that they experienced a conversion and were "born again," he explains. "We refocused our marriage and our lives toward living a Christian life and what that really meant," he says. "How do you live a Christian life if you don't give back – through doing and being involved and engaged?"

His involvement with Rainbow Network has also shown him what success should look like if that organization is truly doing God's work. It would mean that the very people being empowered by Rainbow Network should ultimately be able to continue that work themselves. "A Rainbow Network led by Nicaraguans" with the U.S. office providing financial support and guidance.

"That would be success for a ministry in any country," he says. "They own it, run it, maintain it and grow it to benefit their own people."

During the next years, Jay is excited to welcome more Nicaraguans on the board, even move board meetings to Nicaragua. "It has to be seen as their organization, serving their people," he says.

Doubling in size the number of communities and people served over the next seven years is another goal for Jay. "The focus should be on how to continue to grow," he says. "Serving more people and touching more lives is part of the organizational goals."

Jay also sees that Rainbow, like Habitat, doesn't just go into a community and build a few houses. It is involved with families for the next 20 years or more. When a Rainbow Network project is started, it makes a commitment to those families for years. That commitment must be met on the local level.

He acknowledges that change is never easy, but all organizations, from those as small as Rainbow Network to as large as General Electric, go through changes. He saw Habitat for Humanity in Springfield go from an all-volunteer board directing its operations to hiring a director and now expanding to include a variety of programs. "It's a big organization now," he says.

"I think that's where Rainbow is at," he adds. It started with a founder who had idealistic goals. "Now it's an organization that supports lives in a variety of ways. We will have to change in the coming years. That's the life cycle we are in now."

It is smiling faces like this that reflect the success of the ministry of Rainbow Network in rural Nicaragua. The goal of doubling that ministry to reach more than 80,000 families seems daunting, but the face of a needy child makes it imperative.

Nelson Palacios directs Rainbow Network operations in Nicaragua. His love for Rainbow Network is expressed in a beautiful song he wrote and sang for the 20th anniversary celebrations.

142

CHAPTER TWENTY-FIVE

LEARNING TO BE A LEADER

Nelson Palacios is now the Nicaragua director of Rainbow Network, but he learned to be a leader from his father when he was just a teenager.

As a young teen, he volunteered to serve as president of a committee in his community to build a school. In 1977, the small school building was erected. A year later, he worked to form a public library in Nagarote, using an area in the local Catholic church. He collected books and formed a lending library the same year he graduated from high school.

"My brother and I were the leaders of that committee," he says. "My father was a leader in the church at that time. He kind of put us up to it."

"After that, the revolution happened," he adds matter-of-factly.

But the Sandinistas also saw his leadership qualities and made him a commandant in the Leon and Nagarote area. He organized young people for the military.

He was only 16 years old.

Asked if he had to fight in the civil war, he answers, "Si," with a sigh. He also lost both of his best friends in the war. Armed with nothing more than a small pistol, Nelson and his friends were camped out in the country, trying to defend the area against the government's National Guard. "It was very difficult, very scary," he says.

In fact, he lost friends on both sides of the battle – the National Guard and the Sandinista rebels.

He was 18 at the time.

That year, 1979, he became the political head of the Sandinistas in one sector. For a year, he organized people for the Sandinistas in Nagarote and La Paz Centro.

"I learned to do Rainbow work and didn't even know it," says Nelson. The irony is not lost on him.

A year later, he traveled to Bulgaria to study European history. When he returned, just 20 years old, his first daughter was born, and he had no job. "I really didn't have anything to do," he says. The revolution had been won, but a civil war – the Sandinistas versus the Contras – was in full swing. Nelson went back to work for the army. "They gave me a battalion of young men," he says. Six months later he returned to his family, then was sent up to the north of the country on another tour of duty. That is when his second daughter was born. "And I wasn't there," he says with a sigh of regret.

At that point, the formal fighting was over, but the paranoia and anxiety were still high. "It was very difficult," Nelson says. "You didn't know who was the enemy and who wasn't. It was very scary."

Nelson and a group of others simply walked away. "I retired from political life and returned as a school teacher," he says.

That was what he was doing when he discovered Rainbow Network. He was a high school teacher in Nagarote, the father of six children. He saw what Rainbow was doing in that network and decided to apply for a job when he learned that Rainbow's education coordinator for Nagarote and Ciudad Sandino had been promoted.

He got the job. His leadership skills paid off, and he was eventually moved up to direct the entire operation.

Now the grandfather of four, he sees a very different life for his family than the one in which he grew up. "We had a lot of difficulties and no money," he says. "My grandchildren now have many possibilities."

While Keith Jaspers was learning leadership skills running his own business and being part of Habitat for Humanity International, Nelson was learning to lead in the middle of a revolution and then a civil war. But, both arrived at the same place – Rainbow Network.

Nelson has taken the organization forward. Despite the economic crisis that struck in 2008 and its impact on the organization, he made sure that the poor people of rural Nicaragua continued to have the support and encouragement they needed to improve their lives and change their country.

As Rainbow Network celebrated 20 years of service in 2015, Nelson shared the story of the organization through song. Nelson sings and plays the guitar with the ease and talent of a professional, and the lyrics he wrote share his heart.

These are some of the words, translated into English, from "Red Arco Iris (Rainbow Network) in Nicaragua:"

"In the year 1995, a light illuminated Nicaragua.
It was Arco Iris that was born near Managua.
The poor with hope were filled with joy
When knowing that soon their lives would change.

To share the love of Christ is the mission statement of Rainbow
With the poorest families of Nicaragua,
Bringing to them health care, micro loans and housing
And education, and so they learn."

The song goes on to thank all the churches and supporters, as well as founder Keith Jaspers and his board of directors, who have made Rainbow Network's work in Nicaragua possible.

At the various celebrations held throughout the networks, Nelson is there, dressed in the traditional colorful Nicaraguan clothes, holding his guitar and singing, often accompanied by young people dancing. The audience is all smiles as it joins in on the chorus.

Like the song, Nelson brings the joy of Rainbow Network to the people of rural Nicaragua.

Keith and Karen Jaspers used their life experiences, from growing up on a farm in Iowa to running successful businesses, and Keith serving on the board of Habitat for Humanity International, to envision an organization that helped the poor to become self-sufficient. That was the vision that became The Rainbow Network.

CHAPTER
TWENTY-SIX

Rainbow Network's History

Perhaps few people expected the ginger-haired boy born to a northern Iowa farm family to become a successful businessman or a personal friend to an ex-president, and certainly no one would have thought he would start an organization that would change thousands of lives in a country more than 3,000 miles away in Central America.

But that is the story of Keith Jaspers and Rainbow Network. Both have grown from modest beginnings to success. Both have struggled through hard times and come out stronger at the other end. And both have put the work of Christ before personal accolades.

Keith grew up on a family farm with hogs, chickens and cattle. He was accustomed to hard work. His wife, Karen, grew up on a farm nearby, the oldest of eight children raised by her mother after her father died young.

It was the 1940s, in the middle of World War II, when Keith and Karen were born.

Far to the south, in Nicaragua, the seeds of a revolution had been planted when, in 1934, revolutionary Augusto Cesar Sandino was assassinated by National Guard commander, General Anastasio Somoza Garcia.

The farmers of northern Iowa, like much of the rest of the United States, knew little about what was happening in Nicaragua. But about 50 years later, these two Iowa farm kids would visit that country, changing their lives and the lives of thousands of Nicaraguans in a profound way.

As the Somoza dictatorship was taking control of Nicaragua, Keith and Karen were growing up, going to college, getting married and starting a family. But life wasn't easy.

"I remember when our first child was born, and all we had between us was some loose change a jar of peanut butter and some crackers," Keith recalls. "It kind of hit us that this is where the fork in the road is.

147

You're either going to go one way or the other, so we buckled down and worked hard. And continue to."

Keith went to work at a Kinney Shoes store, where a persistent sales pitch turned into an opportunity.

"I sold a pair of shoes to a gentleman who was all dressed up," he remembers. "I sold him arch supports, a pair of socks and a can of shoe polish."

When the young father walked out of work that night, that gentleman was waiting outside with an offer. He was the district manager for Osco Drugs next door and he hired Keith on the spot for a management training program.

Five years and three cities later, the Jaspers family had three children and Keith was working 70 hours a week.

Soon he embraced a new challenge in the fledgling telemarketing business – selling Sathers cookies and candies over the phone.

"This guy decided we could sell things over the telephone," Keith explains about the career choice that occupied the next nine years of his life. "We sold a lot. Nobody was selling by phone at that time."

While Americans were buying cookies by phone, Nicaragua was devastated by an earthquake that killed at least 5,000 people. It was not the first natural or man-made disaster to hit the country, and it would not be the last.

By 1978, Keith and Karen were ready to try their hands at their own business – a run-down bowling alley in Worthington, Minnesota.

"I had never bowled a game in my life," Keith admits, without even a hint of a smile. "But I could add and subtract pretty good, and I figured out that if you sold a game of bowling you didn't have to buy one back at wholesale. I didn't have much money, but if I could keep selling a game of bowling over and over, I figured a guy ought to be able to make money doing that."

In four years, they sold the bowling alley and doubled their investment. That is when they moved to Springfield, Missouri, where they bought another bowling alley. Five years later, they sold the bowling alley and went into the hotel business.

While Keith and Karen were learning how to be successful entrepreneurs, Nicaragua was learning how to lead a revolution. In 1980, the last Somoza dictator was assassinated and the Sandinista revolution set up its government, led by a young revolutionary named Daniel Ortega.

As the Jaspers were moving to Springfield, U.S.-sponsored Contra rebels began attacking the Sandinistas. The government declared a state of emergency and the civil war that would further devastate Nicaragua began in earnest.

* * *

Sharing Success

Keith and Karen had decided many years earlier that if they ever accomplished financial success, they would find a way to share. "If we were well with our families and our own lives and had the excess finances to start something and help other people, that was just the thing to do," Keith says.

It was 1982 when Keith and Karen read the book "Love in the Mortar Joints" by Millard Fuller, the founder of Habitat for Humanity. Curious, the couple drove from Minnesota to Americus, Georgia, where Habitat was headquartered, "to see what they did down there and how they did it."

A year later – 40 years old at the time – Keith was sitting next to former President Jimmy Carter and author-theologian Tony Campolo on the Habitat for Humanity International board. He served on the board for seven years, then on several committees until 1996.

"I've had such wonderful opportunities to learn and grow working with those people," Keith says. "Rainbow is what it is today because of what I learned."

He learned that he could love his neighbor through his business experience and let his actions speak louder than any words he could preach.

"The way I understand the Bible, as Christians, we should help people, especially the poor. There are hundreds of references to that in the New Testament," Keith says.

He came up with a plan to use his own money and business acumen to "do unto others."

There were three criteria: the work had to be something that wouldn't otherwise happen if they didn't do it, the community served had to take an active role and invite them to help, the mission had to be close enough to get there in a day.

The flight to Managua, Nicaragua, is about six hours.

As Keith and Karen were learning how to "do unto others," the poor families of rural Nicaragua were suffering through a civil war, a hurricane and another earthquake. Their government was embroiled in its own battles and did little for these poor people. Even the capital city of Managua was left in rubble.

That is the Nicaragua that Keith saw when he arrived at the airport in Managua in the mid-1980s with Millard and Linda Fuller to start a Habitat for Humanity project.

"That's when I first saw the poverty," he recalls.

Keith also traveled to Haiti with Habitat, and it was there that he first believed God was leading him to do his own project. However, God had other plans. Just as he was about to get started, he learned that Haiti had been awarded a $2.5 million grant from the European Union for a similar effort.

The trip to Nicaragua was still fresh in his mind. He felt God had planted that seed, and Keith was going to water it. He met with local churches and talked about his ideas, getting encouragement along the way. With spiritual support, he and Karen began the project, funded entirely by their own money.

Friends proposed that the new organization be named for its founders, but Keith and Karen preferred to remain in the background. They did not want to put themselves ahead of God, so instead they chose a name that reflected "God's promise of hope and protection."

The rainbow story in Genesis reflects that promise.

Once the foundation became public and invited others to be part of it, he found that it was the right decision.

"The second part of the name – Network – has many layers of meaning," Keith explains. It reflects the "economy of management by combining the four areas of service into one office. It's part of our efficiencies – networking them together."

It also represents the way that donors and partners "are networking with the Nicaraguans who receive" the help, Keith says. "All of it, as a whole, networks with donors and churches here. They go down as partners to network" with the Nicaraguan staff and the recipients.

The mission field was found and the name selected. Now the mission needed to be established.

In 1996, the year after Rainbow Network was founded, the civil war was finally over in Nicaragua and the Jaspers were ready to work. Keith went to Nicaragua to tour the countryside where they felt the need was greatest and they could achieve their goal of empowering people to succeed through a holistic support system that first addressed basic needs of healthcare and education, then added housing and economic development.

They held community meetings, learning the needs and trying to design projects that would work. A year earlier, they had hired a director to get things ready. Peter Schaller, an American who had moved to Nicaragua, married and started a family there. He was able to be a bridge between the Nicaraguans and the U.S. patrons. He hired local people to help coordinate the education program and a medical doctor.

With Peter's help and the assistance of some U.S. missionaries in Nicaragua, Keith and Karen settled on the community of Ciudad Sandino as the first "network."

"The need was just overwhelming," Keith said. "The people were living in desperate poverty and nobody was helping them." There were no elementary schools there, no medical care, no jobs, no banks. Nearly everyone was living in some version of a plastic and scrap home, taped and wired together, with dirt floors.

"When I met with the people, they were very anxious to work with someone, but they also had been promised things from other organizations that never delivered," he recalls.

The people of Ciudad Sandino had proved themselves willing and able to participate in the program – one of the requirements for Keith and Karen – but now Rainbow Network had to prove itself to the people of Ciudad Sandino.

"Missionaries go down with good hearts and good intentions, but they have no money and no support to do anything," Keith says.

That is what made Rainbow Network different. With Keith and Karen's financial commitment, they were assured that the work would be done. They established the Ciudad Sandino network, with its five rural villages outside the town.

"People were just ecstatic," Keith remembers. "We were saving lives." He recalls seeing a man on the examining table seriously ill, near death. He was given a shot of ampicillin. The next time Keith saw the man he was sitting in the dentist's chair, otherwise healthy.

In addition to medical clinics, Rainbow Network schools were started in each community. About a year later, housing was added. The first project was 15 houses in Filos de Cuajachillo. Today, it is still a thriving project – and all the houses are paid for!

Keith and Karen wanted to be confident that the plan was working before adding more communities. Working slowly, holding town hall meetings and setting up committees, local leaders began to emerge. This was evidence that Rainbow Network was succeeding in empowering Nicaraguans to lead themselves.

But there were still lessons to learn.

* * *

Feeding the Hungry

One day, Keith was at a daylong meeting in Trinidad Central. It was late in the day, and he was tired, looking forward to getting back to his hotel for dinner and going to bed so he would be ready for an early morning flight home the next day.

"I was looking at my watch, as any important U.S. executive ought to be," he says with obvious sarcasm. "Then a school teacher very timidly raised her hand. 'One more thing, Señor,' she said. 'I do have several children in my classroom that are actually fainting every day because of hunger.'"

Keith had been learning Spanish and thought he understood what she had said, but he had to ask his translator to be sure he had heard her correctly.

"We sat back down and started the meeting over again," he said. "Then we started the feeding centers the next week or so. We still operate 136 feeding centers, but at our peak we had 212."

Hunger and poverty never seem to disappear, but through the Rainbow Network programs, people have been able to support their families so that malnutrition is rare in Rainbow communities. In some areas, feeding centers, which are held at the local elementary school at lunchtime, are now only needed during the dry season when family gardens can't produce enough. And fewer children need the extra nutrition in many of the established communities. Pregnant and nursing mothers, as well as the sick and elderly, are also welcome to eat lunch at the centers, and the Rainbow doctors will sometimes prescribe the meal.

About a year after starting the Ciudad Sandino network, the scholarship program began. Until then, all the emphasis had been on the elementary level, making sure everyone could read and write and had basic skills. But it came to Keith's attention that, after the sixth grade, there were few opportunities for a secondary education. There were no high schools in the rural areas, so a scholarship program was established to send students to the nearest city to school. It started with about 15 students. "Now we have over 1,000 kids in that program," Keith says with pride. "We have graduated more than 1,500 students through our scholarship program."

Micro loans were part of the original plan for Rainbow Network, but it was important to first get acquainted with the people and establish a working relationship. About six months after arriving in Ciudad Sandino, the first small loans were given. Now, more than 4,000 families have loans out at any given time throughout all of the networks.

Building a program like Rainbow Network takes time as workable solutions are found and needs are resolved. As Nicaragua was struggling to find its own solutions, Rainbow Network was responding to immediate and long term needs in its communities.

Water was one of those needs. In many communities it was common for people to drink surface water or from creeks. Drinking polluted water was making people sick. Rainbow worked with several other organizations to drill at least 50 wells in the past 20 years. Waterlines were hooked up to about another 50 communities.

All of the Rainbow housing projects, as well as another 50 communities in the networks, have potable water available.

Electricity is another need. Rainbow Network will pay to bring electricity into its housing projects, but not to the communities around them. However, because Rainbow does such great work, providing housing, medical care and education, the municipal government is often motivated to run power lines to existing communities. "That has happened at least 50 times," Keith says.

The rural poor of Nicaragua rarely see a dentist, and then only if the pain is so great that they opt for an extraction. So, for the first years after Rainbow started, dental brigades from the United States were brought down, doing extensive dental work at their own expense.

"They were heroes," Keith says, especially of Dr. Ed Schanda and Dr. Chris Willard, who also trained local dentists and financed the early dental clinics. Rainbow still has a dental clinic in each of the network offices, with local dentists who travel to each of the seven locations.

When Rainbow began, there was a lot of need for training. For example, some of the women were taught how to sew professionally, and sewing cooperatives were established with donated sewing machines. Safe, effective farming practices were taught, as well as financial planning and accounting. In some cases, such as raising chickens, a manual was developed with clear directions on when to give antibiotics or which feed to use, when the chickens are ready for slaughter, and then pictures showing how to do it. If someone received a Rainbow loan to raise chickens, it was required that they follow the directions, which would all but guarantee success.

But 20 years later, that outside training and direct supervision is rarely needed. Part of the agreement with Rainbow Network is that local residents will train each other. For example, in Valle de San Juan a handful of families made hammocks, passing their knowledge down from generation to generation. Now, they pass it along to neighbors, too. Today, there are 150 families in Valle de San Juan that make a living making and selling hammocks throughout the region.

"Once you've got two or three people in the community that know how to do something, whether it is making a shirt or butchering a cow, we expect them to answer others' questions," Keith explains. "If you are with Rainbow, you have to share your knowledge."

While all the Rainbow programs are important to the overall success of Rainbow Network, Keith credits the micro loans and the housing projects as "changing lives permanently and forever."

"With an average of eight people living in each house, the 1,000 homes built by Rainbow since it started in Ciudad Sandino have provided 8,000 people with a safe, secure home, instead of a mud hut," Keith says. "And the thousands of loans being made mean thousands of families are making enough money to begin to lift out of poverty."

But then Keith stops. "Of course, there is the education program," he adds. "Mothers in Nicaragua want the same things for their kids as we want for our kids. That high school sponsorship program, in many ways is the most popular thing that we do with a lot of families. Mom and Dad really want that for their kids."

Rainbow Network recognizes that working one's way out of poverty can be an impossibility, especially when hunger, illness, illiteracy, fear and hopelessness greet Nicaraguan families every day. Giving those families the tools they need to change their lives has not only impacted the families in the programs, but it has changed the lives around them as they spread their knowledge and their success.

Americans like to think that true success is pulling yourself up by your own bootstraps. Rainbow Network is simply providing the bootstraps.

The men and women of rural Nicaragua have been praying to God to send help for their families, help to feed their children, give them access to education and a better future. They insist that God has answered their prayers. God sent Rainbow Network.

CHAPTER
TWENTY-SEVEN

How You Can Help

You have read about the many ways that individuals, churches, businesses, foundations and other organizations can get involved and support Rainbow Network and the work it is doing in rural Nicaragua.

But, as Rainbow Network expands and becomes a larger and more influential presence for God's love in Central America, an army is needed – an army of prayer warriors who will keep the ministry and the people of Nicaragua in their hearts and lift them up to the Lord.

It is only God, through the diligent work and support of those who feel called to do God's work with the poor, who can sustain Rainbow Network and lead the organization.

The work Rainbow Network does in rural Nicaragua takes money. It takes hands-on involvement of the Rainbow staff. It takes old-fashioned grit and elbow grease on the part of participants.

But it also takes you – your prayers, your witness, your support and stewardship. Rainbow Network needs people to share the story of the poor in rural Nicaragua and the work God is doing there. Rainbow needs people to spread the word about the joy of being God's hands and feet to get that work done.

You have read the stories of people, in the United States and in Nicaragua, who have been led by God to step out in faith. Some did it through financial support, some traveled all the way to Nicaragua to personally touch the people they were helping and some gave up careers to serve as Rainbow staff.

Many more people are supporting Rainbow Network through small monthly donations, daily prayers and constant love.

If this book has touched your heart, you can purchase a few more copies to pass along to your friends or others you think would have their hearts opened by it. Churches and Sunday School classes can purchase the books to share with members.

If this is the first look you have had at the need and the work being done through Rainbow Network, you are invited to learn even more. You can contact the Rainbow Network office in Springfield, Missouri, by phone or online, to get more information. You can invite a Rainbow Network representative to your church or organization to tell the story. You can go on a "Go & See" visit to Nicaragua.

God will do the rest. God will touch the hearts that are open, lead each heart to take the action that is meant for them and use each soul to make the change that is needed.

The need is great, but nothing is too hard for God.

* * *

To learn more about Rainbow Network or to get more copies of this book, visit us online:

www.RainbowNetwork.org

or call the office in Springfield, Missouri:

(417) 889 8088

You can also write to us:

The Rainbow Network
2840 East Chestnut Expressway
Suite A
Springfield, MO 65802